DRAWING Fantasy CHIBI

LEARN HOW TO DRAW
Kawaii Unicorns, Mermaids, Dragons, and Other Mythical, Magical Creatures

Illustrations by Tessa Creative Art
Text by Sarah E. White

Published by:
Bloom Books for Young Readers,
an imprint of Ulysses Press
PO Box 3440
Berkeley, CA 94703
www.ulyssespress.com

ISBN: 978-1-64604-402-3
Library of Congress Control Number: 2022936263

Printed in Canada by Marquis Book Printing
10 9 8 7 6 5 4 3 2 1

Acquisitions editor: Kierra Sondereker
Managing editor: Claire Chun
Editor: Renee Rutledge
Proofreader: Joyce Wu
Front cover design and illustrations: Fiverr
Interior design and layout: Winnie Liu

CONTENTS

FANTASY HUMANOID CREATURES

Gnomes are famous for hanging out in gardens, often underground, and are known for being clever, mischievous and, of course, short. This colorful little guy is easy to draw and fun to decorate in lots of different ways.

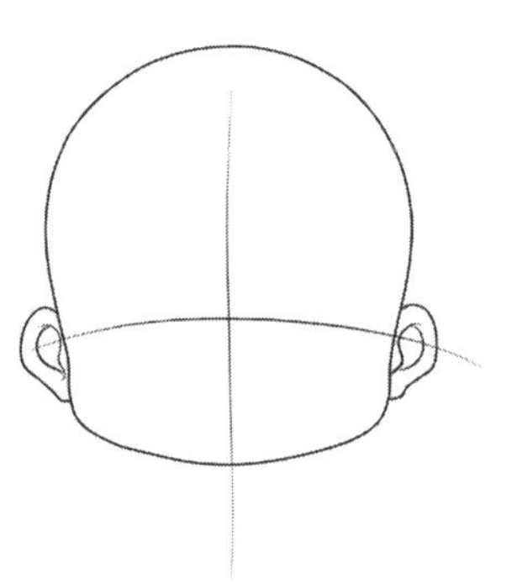

STEP 1

Make the gnome head round at the top and mostly straight down the sides, with a shallow curve along the bottom. Draw a vertical guideline in the middle of the head, and a horizontal one about a third of the way from the bottom. Add ears if you'd like to, though his beard will cover them up later.

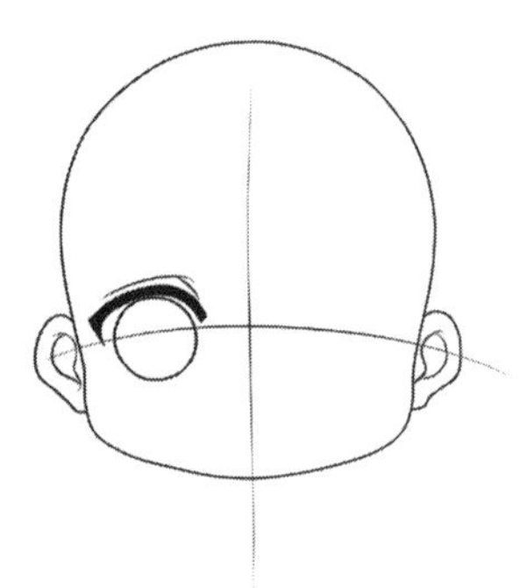

STEP 2

Add a round eye on the left side of the face, with a darker line at the top for the eyelashes.

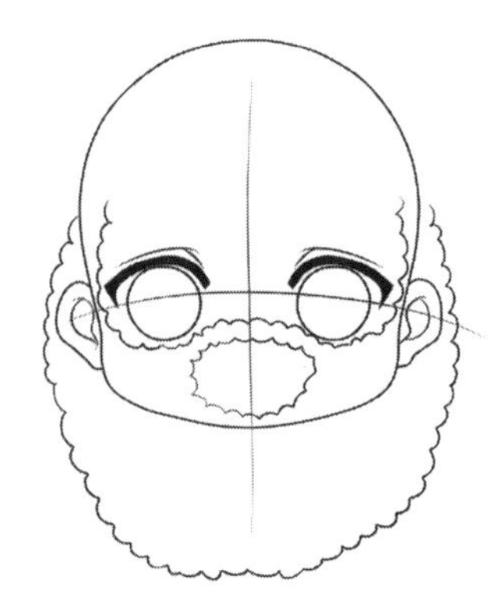

STEP 3

Repeat on the other side. Sketch a half circle where the mouth will go and a large beard underneath the bottom of the face.

STEP 4

Draw a stocking cap with a pompom on top of the head. Add thin, arching eyebrows over the eyes.

STEP 5

Complete the beard so that it covers the sides and bottom of the face. Don't forget a little mustache above the mouth, which is another oval inside the first oval. Draw the rest of the stocking cap so it covers the forehead. Add a slightly curved rectangular shape below the beard to be the gnome's shirt.

STEP 6

Make two smaller rectangles below the first to make the gnome's pants.

STEP 7

Add stripes to the shirt to make his belt.

STEP 8

Erase the guidelines and add details to eyes. Add sleeves to the shirt and little human-like hands. Draw curved shoes below the pants.

Practice drawing the gnome below!

Keep going from step 1.

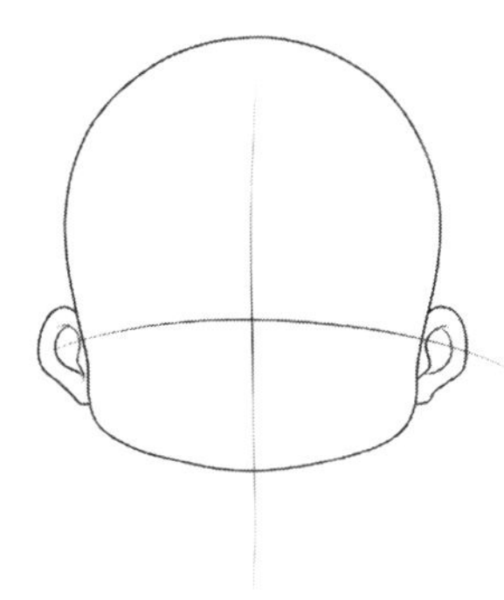

Try a few from scratch.

DWARF

Dwarves are short but strong and usually skilled in crafts like mining and forging. This dwarf has a large tool—maybe a hammer?—as he's heading off to work soon, but you can leave that part out of the drawing if you'd rather just have a cute little character.

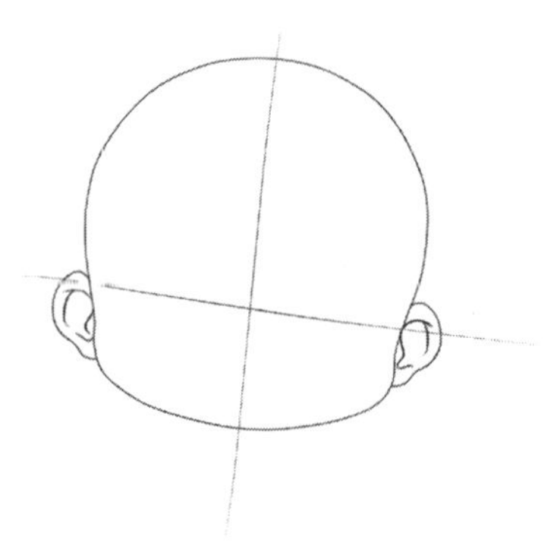

STEP 1 Start with a circle that's pinched flat on the sides to form the head. Draw a vertical guideline down the middle and a horizontal one about two thirds of the way down the face. You can draw ears just below the horizontal guideline, but they'll be covered by hair before long.

STEP 2 Sketch the beginnings of the hair by drawing a circle around the whole head and making a hairline that looks like a V. Add lines for the beard, which is cinched up here like a ponytail, at the center bottom of the face. Draw a round eye on the horizontal line on the right side of the face, close to the vertical line. Make the top darker than the bottom.

STEP 3

Repeat the eye on the left side of the face and add eyebrows. Draw a small dome-shaped beanie at the top of the head, a little left of center. Make the shirt by drawing three sides of a square coming down around the center bottom of the head.

STEP 4

Add a fancy mustache under the eyes. The jacket, pants, and belt are mostly rectangles and squares. Draw the jacket so the left arm is raised and the right arm is lowered.

STEP 5

Draw short arms and hands, with fingers closed. Add a tiny bit of leg and slightly rounded rectangles for boots. Make a small half circle under the mustache for a mouth.

STEP 6

Give your dwarf a hammer by drawing a handle in his hand and two sides of a rectangle on top going behind his head on the left. The top of the tool is curved and has two lines.

STEP 7

Draw an X on the tool for the straps that hold it together.

STEP 8

Erase the guidelines and add details to eyes and blush on the cheeks.

Practice drawing the dwarf below!

Keep going from step 1.

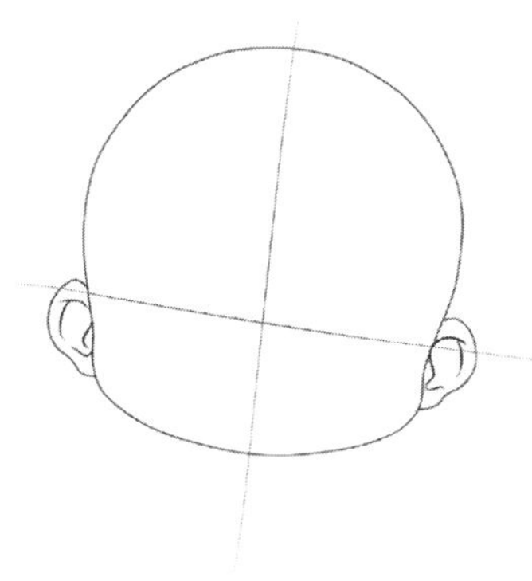

Try a few from scratch.

ONI

An oni is a demon from Japanese folklore, and it's usually depicted with horns, wild hair, and fangs. They can have different skin colors, so you can make yours red, blue, green, or any color you like. This version wields a spade-like spear, but they are often shown carrying clubs, so there are lots of options for changing this easy design.

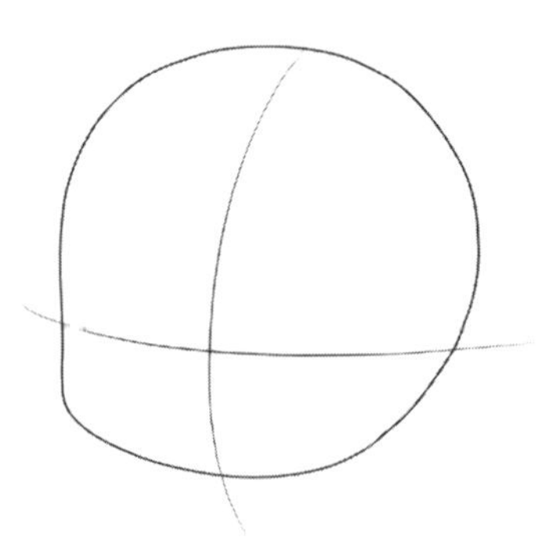

STEP 1 Start with a mostly round head, with guidelines dividing the head in half vertically and about a third of the way from the bottom horizontally.

STEP 2 Draw an eye on the right side of the face along the horizontal line. Add a heavier arched line just above the eye. Make a short neck and draw the top of the oni's robe and belt.

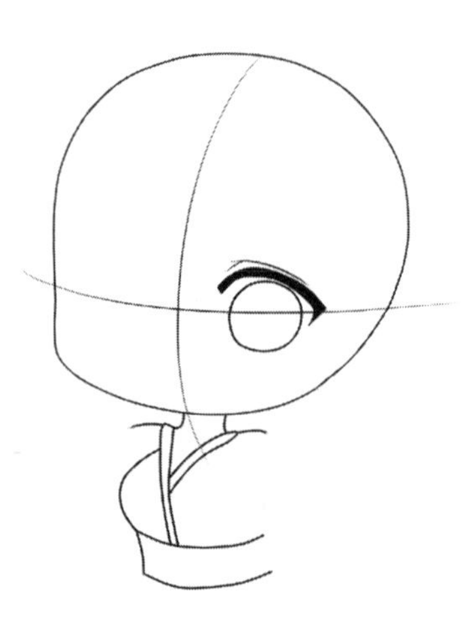

STEP 3

Add an eye on the left side. Draw curved rectangle shapes for the sides of the robe, with a little line between them for the garment under the robe.

STEP 4

Sketch long bangs in three pointed sections and long hair flowing over the right shoulder. Add legs—right leg in front of the left—and a curve at the end of the leg for the slipper. Sketch high eyebrows over the eyes.

STEP 5

Draw rectangular sleeves joining to the top of the robe, and add hair on the left side. Make a half circle below and between the eyes for the mouth, with two tiny triangles for fangs, and add a triangular ear below the horizontal guideline on the right side of the face.

STEP 6

Add curved triangular horns at the top of the head and small hands at the ends of the robe sleeves. The left hand in this example has curled-under fingers and the right hand is open, palm facing back.

STEP 7

Draw the stick part of the spear the oni is holding. It's wider at the top and tapers down toward the hand.

STEP 8

Add a large triangle to the end of the stick, pointing down. If desired, add a little tail with a triangle on the end. Erase the guidelines and add details to eyes and blush on the cheeks, and tiny little teeth.

Practice drawing the oni below!

Keep going from step 1.

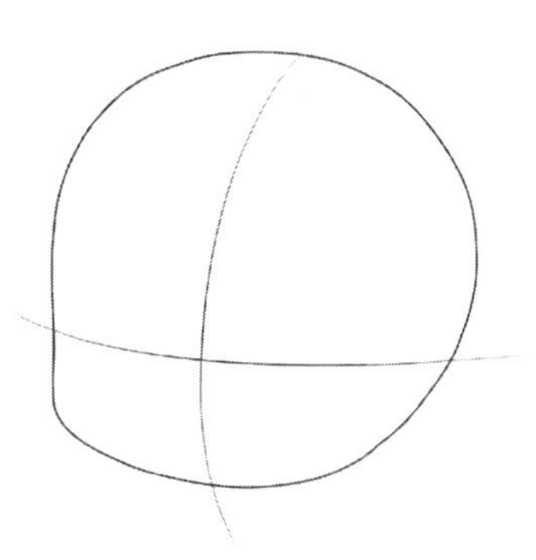

Try a few from scratch.

CYCLOPS

The Cyclops is famously known as having only one eye, and our version is super cute with an eye that takes up most of its face. The monochromatic color scheme is sweet, too, or go bolder and have hair and clothing that are a different color from the eye.

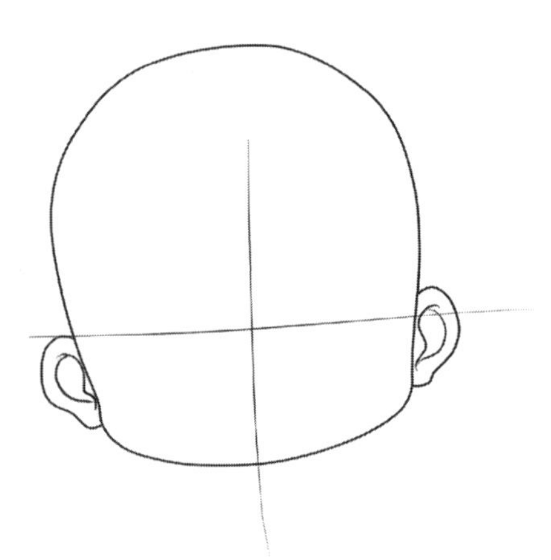

STEP 1 Our Cyclops has a large blocky head with a curve at the top. Mark a vertical guideline down the middle and a horizontal guideline about a third of the way up the head. If you want, you can draw ears beneath the horizontal guideline on the sides of the head, but the hair will cover them up.

STEP 2 The eye is the main feature of the Cyclops, so let's start there. It should be large and round and centered on the guidelines. Add a darker curved line around the top of the eye to give it depth, and add some eyelashes.

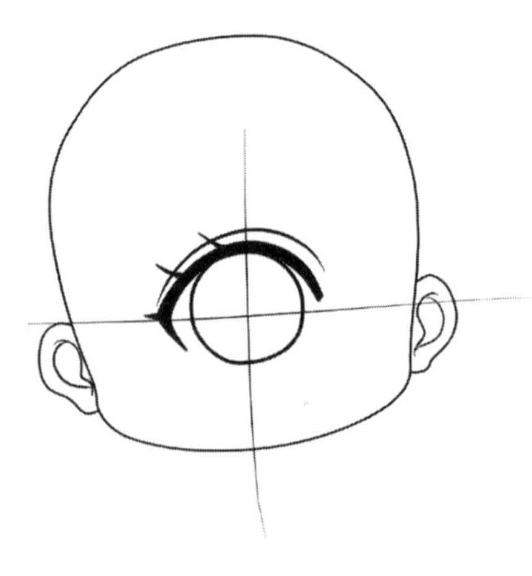

STEP 3 Sketch small triangular horns near the front of the head on the sides, and add a single long eyebrow over the eye. Draw a short neck and tiny shoulders, and the bodice for the top.

STEP 4 Add a frilly skirt below the bodice. The sides are diagonal lines while the bottom is ruffled. Make a straight line very low on the face for the mouth.

STEP 5

Draw short arms with human hands. In this example, the hands are open, with the palms facing back.

STEP 6

Begin to sketch in hair. This Cyclops has very long, wavy hair and bangs. For now, draw in the bands and begin to sketch the hair around the horns and down the left side. Add a short leg, with a little shoe at the end on the left side.

STEP 7 Add the second leg and foot and more hair on the right side.

STEP 8 Erase the guidelines and add detail to the eye. Make the hair as long as you want.

Practice drawing the Cyclops below!

Keep going from step 1.

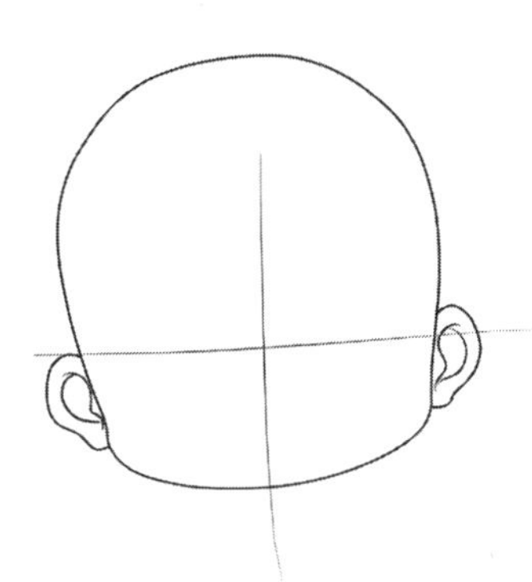

Try a few from scratch.

FAIRY

Fairies are fun to draw because you can give them so many different personalities based on the colors you use and accessories you choose. There are all sorts of options: pastel colored with stars in their hair, forest colored with leaves instead of stars, a beach fairy, or whatever else you can imagine.

STEP 1 Start with a human-style head, round across the top, with straight sides and a smaller curve at the bottom. The vertical guideline should be straight down the middle, while the horizontal line should be about a third of the way up the face.

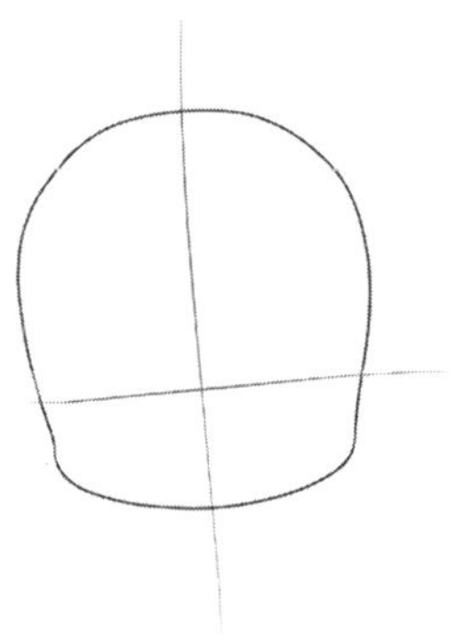

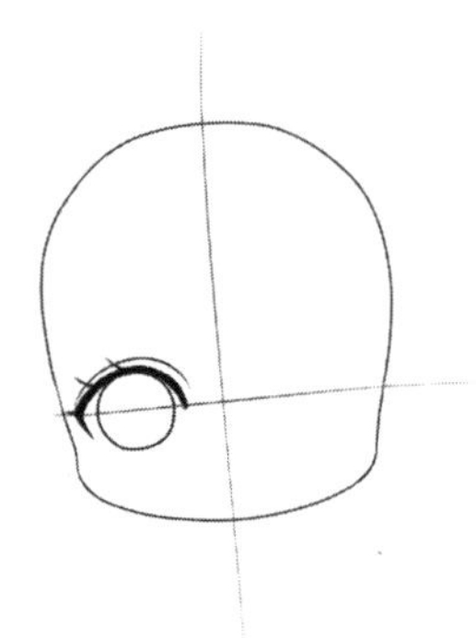

STEP 2 Add a large eye on the left side of the face, centered on the horizontal guideline. Make the top darker than the bottom to indicate eyelashes.

STEP 3 Repeat on the right side, then draw a tiny torso shaped like the body of a bowling pin.

STEP 4 Draw ringlets of hair past the fairy's shoulders, and add bangs and tiny eyebrows behind the bangs. Make the skirt two layers of petals.

STEP 5 Make circles at the top sides of the head for fairy buns. Draw short arms with human fingers. In this example, both hands are open, with palms facing back. Add a line for the mouth.

STEP 6

Now it's time to add little legs and feet, and the top half of the wings, which are upside down and teardrop shaped.

STEP 7

Finish the wings with two pieces that hang down. Add the bodice to the fairy's dress, and a tiny necklace. Include a set of elf-like ears.

STEP 8 Add details to the wings and stars to the hair. Erase the guidelines and finish the eyes.

Practice drawing the fairy below!

Keep going from step 1.

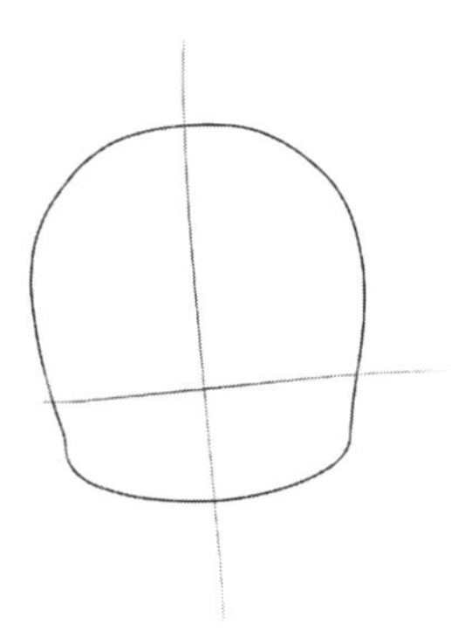

Try a few from scratch.

TROLL

Trolls are not usually known for their cuteness, but this little creature might change your opinion. It looks a little alien with its pointy ears, but you can also draw it with more human-like ears and hair if you like that version better.

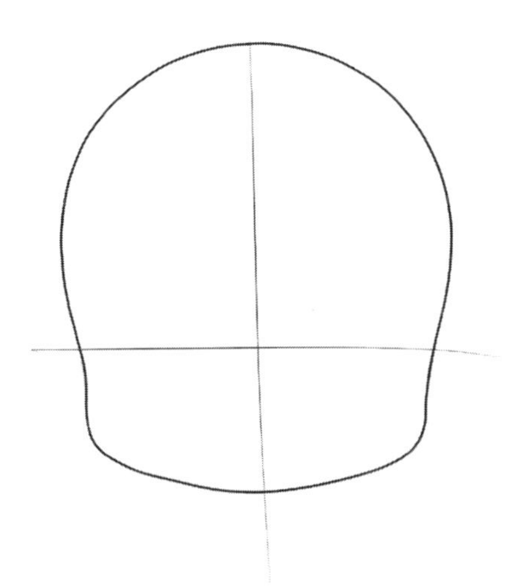

STEP 1 Start by drawing a large circle with the lower sides pinched in a bit. Add a vertical guideline at the center of the circle and a horizontal one about a third of the way up the head, where the pinched part starts.

STEP 2 Draw a large round eye on the left side, centered on the horizontal line. Add a heavy arched line over the eye.

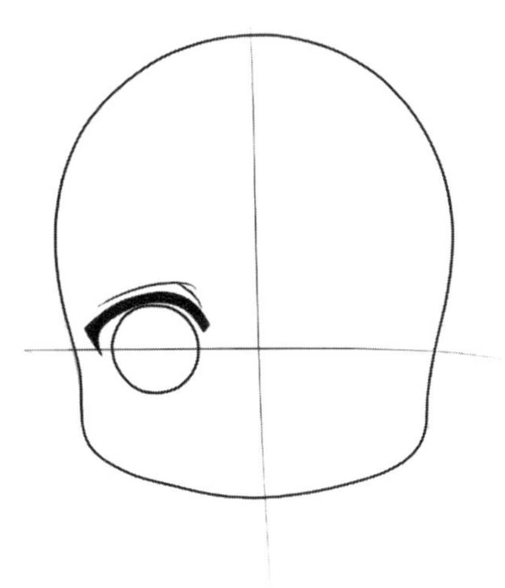

STEP 3

Repeat on the right side, then draw a pointy ear on the left side where the flat part of the face is.

STEP 4

Add an ear to the right side and a high arching eyebrow over the right eye.

STEP 5

Draw another eyebrow over the left eye, then a very short neck and a rectangular body.

STEP 6 Our troll is waving, so one arm will be up and one down. The hand on the left is open with palm out, while the one on the right is open and palm back. Draw a little pair of shorts as a wavy rectangle with a small notch cut out between the legs. Don't forget a large half circle for the mouth.

STEP 7 Add a short leg and a large foot on the left side. Give this troll a necklace—a circle on a chain.

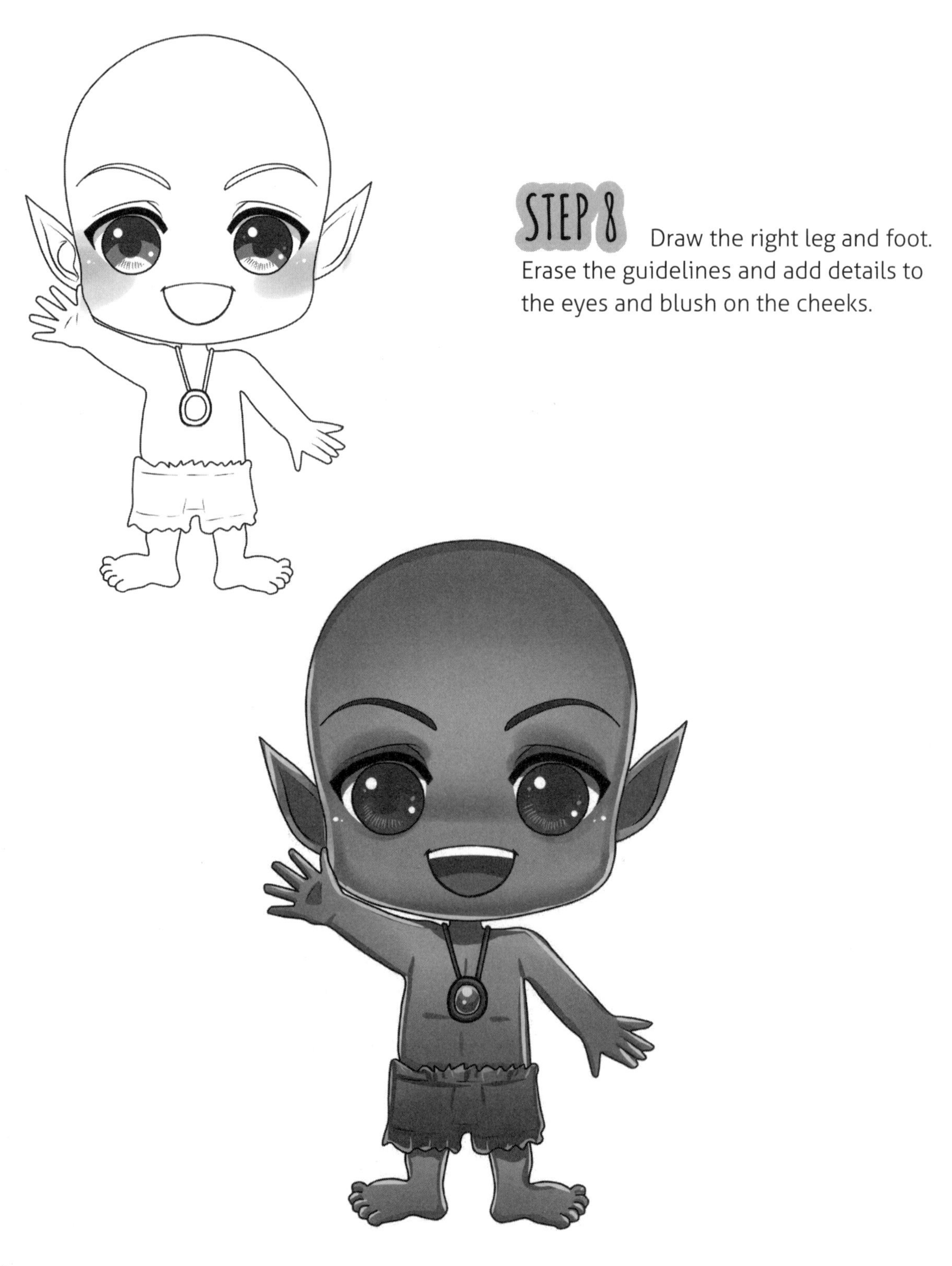

STEP 8

Draw the right leg and foot. Erase the guidelines and add details to the eyes and blush on the cheeks.

Practice drawing the troll below!

Keep going from step 1.

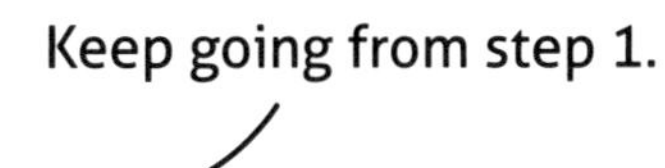

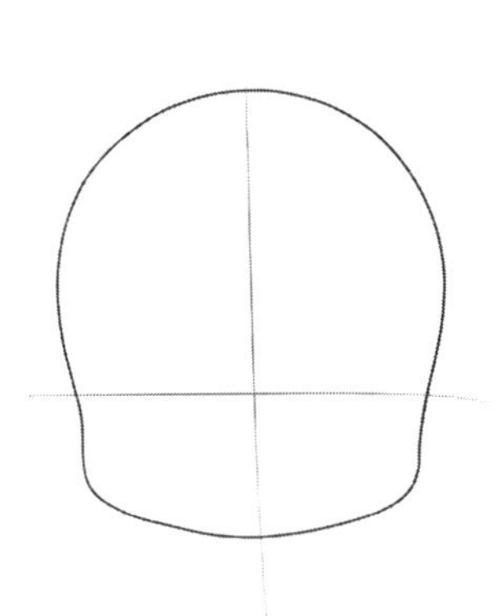

Try a few from scratch.

MEDUSA

Our Medusa takes the mythology a step further and gives her a snake body as well as snake hair. Medusa is a lot of fun to draw because her head is covered with slithering (though, in this case, also adorable) snakes. Add as many as you'd like to give her a dramatic crown. Just don't look her in the eyes!

STEP 1 Medusa's head is mostly circular with a little bit that's straight on the left side. Draw a guideline up the middle vertically and about a quarter of the way up horizontally. Optional: draw ears (they will be mostly covered by snakes eventually).

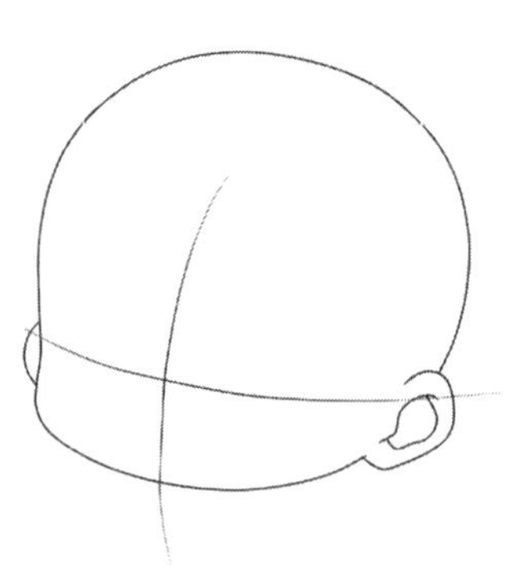

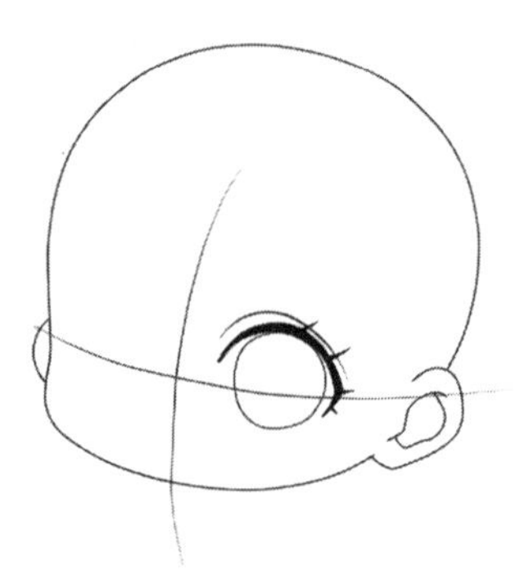

STEP 2 Draw an eye on the right side, a little higher than the horizontal guideline. Add a dark line across the top to give it depth, then add some eyelashes..

STEP 3 Repeat on the left side, then draw little curved lines for Medusa's shoulders and the top of her bodice.

STEP 4 Sketch long curving eyebrows just over the eyes. Add short arms. Our Medusa is waving with her left hand, while her right hand points down.

STEP 5 Next, go wild with the snakes on Medusa's head. Each head is circular at the top and triangular at the bottom. Draw as many as you like as close or as far away from the main head as you see fit. For reference, this example shows ten. Also draw curving lines out from the bodice to begin to form Medusa's snake body. Add a half circle mouth.

STEP 6

Give all the snake heads eyes. If they are not all facing front, make sure you only put one eye on those that are turned. Add a snake tail behind the curve of body you drew in the last step, and draw lines along the body to mark out the center of the body.

STEP 7

Attach the snake heads to Medusa by giving them each a body. Add a forked tongue to her mouth. Mark horizontal lines along the center part of Medusa's body.

STEP 8 Give all the snakes tongues, and segment the center of their bodies, too, if you'd like to. Erase the guidelines and add details to eyes and blush to cheeks.

Practice drawing Medusa below!

Keep going from step 1.

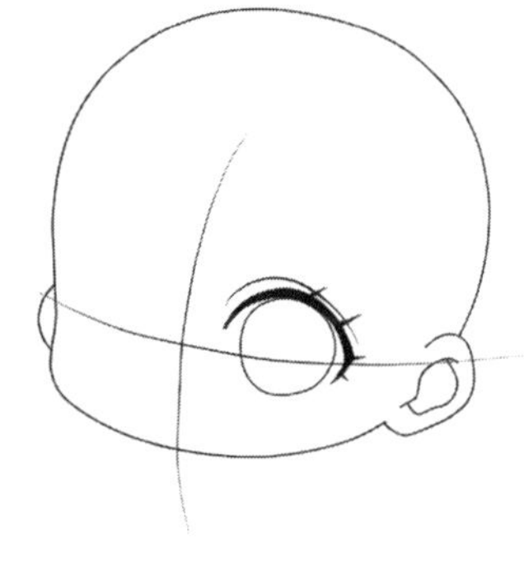

Try a few from scratch.

ELF

There are all sorts of elves out there, from the arrow-wielding elves of high fantasy to holiday elves in shopping malls. This elf is a creature of the forest, blending in with the trees.

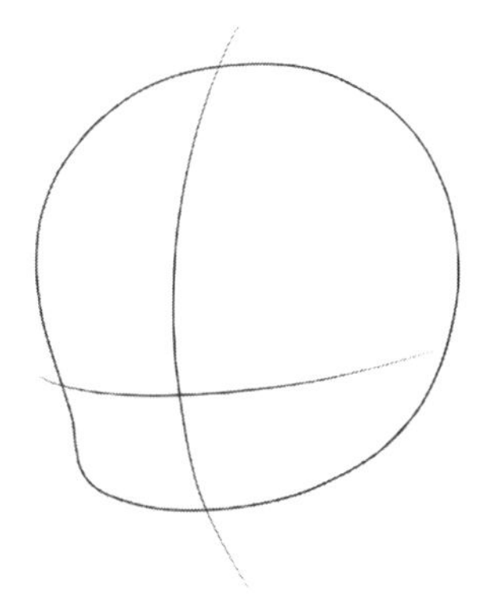

STEP 1 Draw a mostly round form for the head. The left side should be a little straighter than the right. Make the guideline down the center vertically and about a third of the way up the face horizontally.

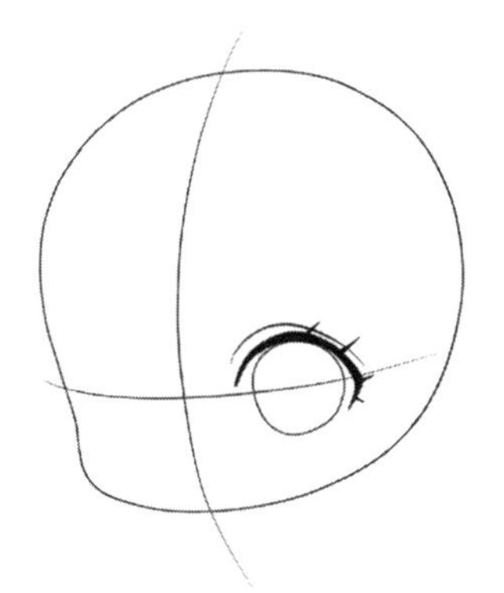

STEP 2 Add a large eye centered on the guideline on the right side of the face. Make the top of the eye darker and add eyelashes.

STEP 3 Repeat on the left side. Draw a small torso that's rectangular, narrowing slightly toward the bottom.

STEP 4 Sketch eyebrows above the eyes. Add short sleeves and embellishments to the top: a tiny V-neck, a curved line at the bodice, and a little belt.

STEP 5 Add arms at the ends of the sleeves, and draw the hands with fingers closed.

STEP 6 Give your elf a braid flowing down the right side of the head past the shoulder. Add bangs as well. Draw a bow in the elf's left hand and a quiver full of arrows on her back, with a sash across her front.

STEP 7 Draw a skirt made of a small rectangle at the center, with longer triangles on each side.

STEP 8 Add a crown of leaves in your elf's hair. Erase the guidelines and add details to the eyes and face. Draw legs, one in front of the other, and long boots.

Practice drawing the elf below!

Keep going from step 1.

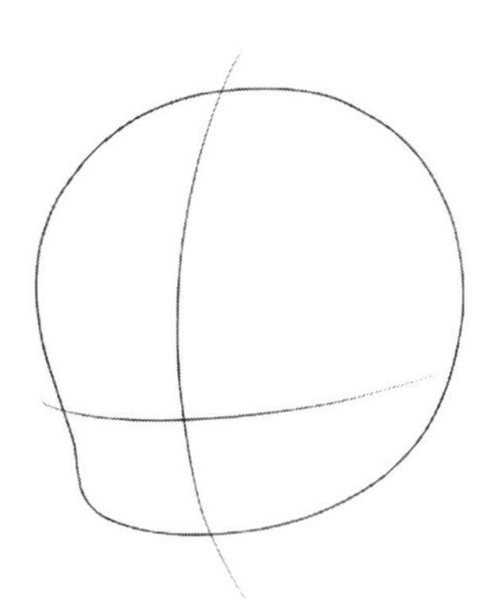

Try a few from scratch.

FANTASY
LAND
CREATURES

UNICORN

Unicorns are easy to make into a chibi because they're already so cute! There are so many options for coloring them in as well. Make matching pastel stripes on its hair, tail, and horn, or make them a solid color or any colors you like. There are no rules when you draw it yourself!

STEP 1 Begin the unicorn's face with straight sides connected with a gentle curve (and small ears) at the top, and a curve at the bottom of the head. Sketch guidelines slightly right of center vertically and just below the center horizontally.

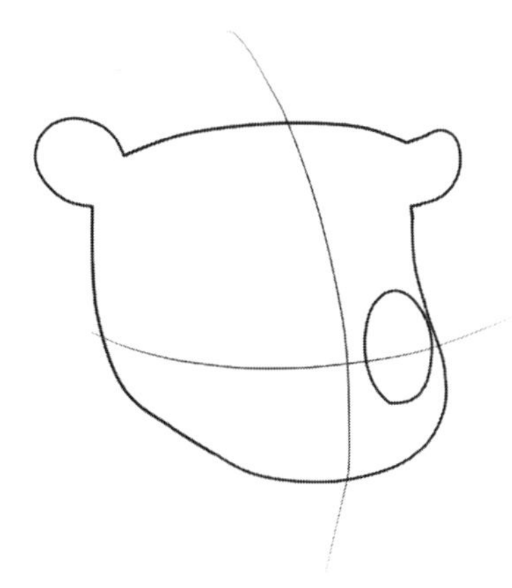

STEP 2 Add an oval for an eye on the right side of the face on the horizontal guideline.

STEP 3 Repeat on the left side, then add sweeping lines for hair between the ears.

STEP 4

Draw a small cone on top of the hair for the horn and add horizontal lines to make stripes. Add an oval on its side for the unicorn's body. Add curving lines to the right sides of the eyes for the whites.

STEP 5

Now it's time for four little legs spaced out around the body. Draw some little eyebrows, too. Erase the back and left side of the face where the unicorn's hair will go.

STEP 6 Draw long, flowing locks on the left side of the face. Draw a little wing on the right side of the unicorn's back, by the face.

STEP 7 Below the wing, sketch out a nice, fluffy tail.

STEP 8 Add lines to the tail and hair so you can color them in different colors. Add eye details. Erase the guidelines.

Practice drawing the unicorn below!

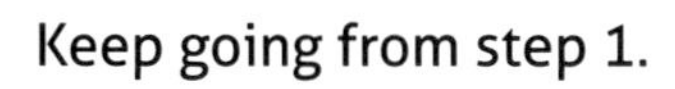

Keep going from step 1.

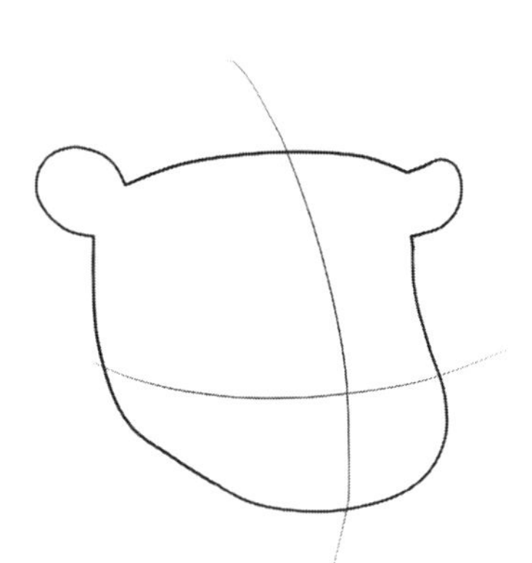

Try a few from scratch.

CATICORN

If there's anything better than a unicorn, it might just be a caticorn. This unicorn with a feline twist is fun to draw. You can go wild with the colors or keep it simple. Don't forget the ball to play with, because it's still a cat, after all.

STEP 1

Start with a cat-shaped face: curved at the bottom with straight sides, triangular ears, and an almost-straight line across the top.

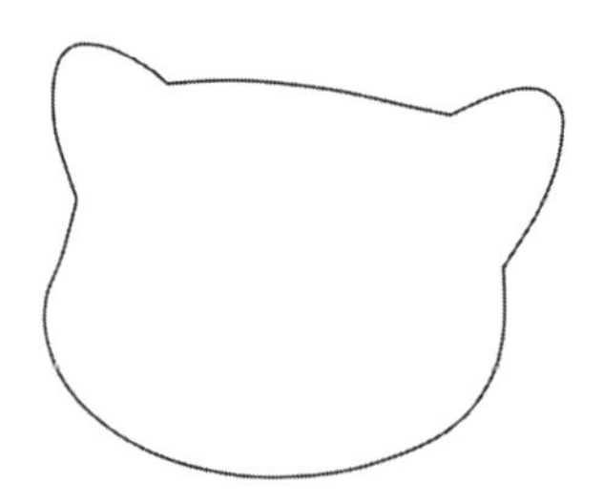

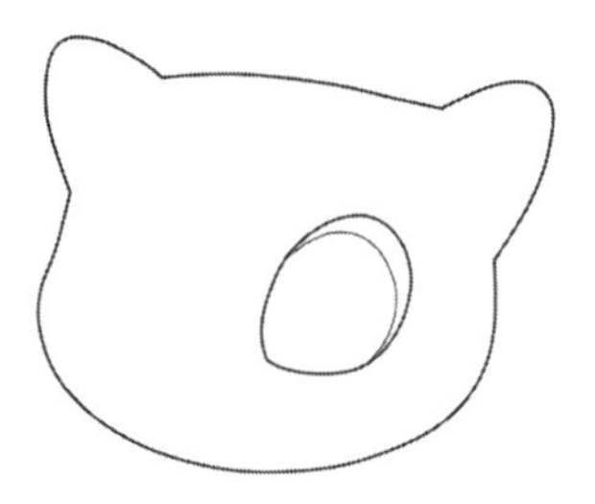

STEP 2

Add an egg-shaped oval slanted slightly toward the center on the right side of the face, with a curve at the top for the white of the eye.

STEP 3

Repeat on the left side. Center small eyebrows over the top of each eye, draw small triangles with wavy bottoms inside the ears, and add lines for the nose and mouth.

STEP 4

Draw a gentle curve starting at the bottom right of the head. Sketch another line with the opposite curve in the space below the first line. These mark the caticorn's body. Add three short lines for whiskers on each side of the face.

STEP 5

Connect the body lines by adding legs and feet. Add another leg behind the first, slightly shorter. The front legs in this example are shorter and open, as if to play with a ball.

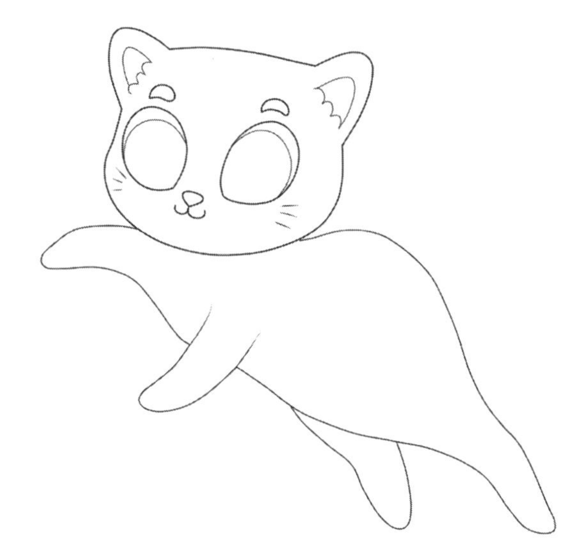

STEP 6

Give your caticorn a big, poofy tail.

STEP 7

Now, add a puffy tuft of hair between the ears, and a ball to play with. Include lines in the hair and tail to allow for adding different colors.

STEP 8

Add a sectioned cone at the center of the top of the head for your caticorn's horn, and add details to the eyes.

Practice drawing the caticorn below!

Keep going from step 1.

Try a few from scratch.

CENTAUR

So many mythical creatures are combinations of other creatures, and the centaur is no exception. Pictured here aiming an arrow, this part horse, part human is all cute.

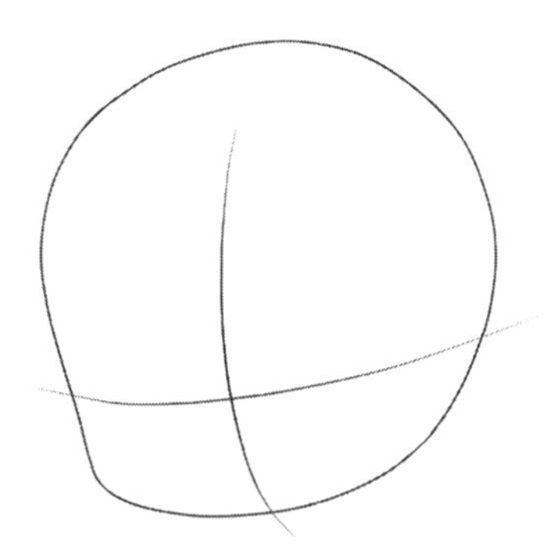

STEP 1 Start at the back of the head, drawing a circle that becomes a straight line on the left side of the head. Draw guidelines up the middle vertically and about a third of the way up from the bottom of the head horizontally.

STEP 2 Make a large circle on the left side of the face on the horizontal guideline. Add a dark line across the top.

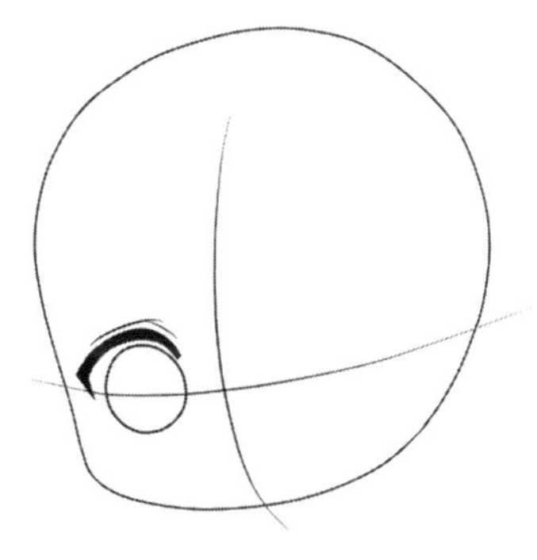

STEP 3 Repeat on the right side, then add a petal-shaped ear at the back right of the head centered on the horizontal guideline.

STEP 4

Draw long, curly bangs that hang down to the eyes. Sketch in eyebrows if desired.

STEP 5

Add more hair around the back of the head flowing down toward the shoulders. Make a horizontal line under the eyes for the centaur's mouth.

STEP 6

Sketch a horse-shaped body that is smaller than the head. The line at the left side of the body starts with a slight diagonal curving down and to the back, while the body at the right side has more of a curve.

STEP 7 Draw little arms with human hands holding a bow and arrow, with the string drawn back so the bow is a triangular shape. Add animal legs, giving the front right leg a little twist for movement.

STEP 8 Erase the guidelines and add details to the eyes and face. Make little mitten shapes at the back of the head for horse ears. Draw a short tail and add hooves to all four feet.

Practice drawing the centaur below!

Keep going from step 1.

Try a few from scratch.

The faun is a creature somewhat similar to a centaur (see page 59), but instead of being a human and horse, this one is a human and goat. We think they would probably be friends, though, so why not draw a forest scene with fauns and centaurs together?

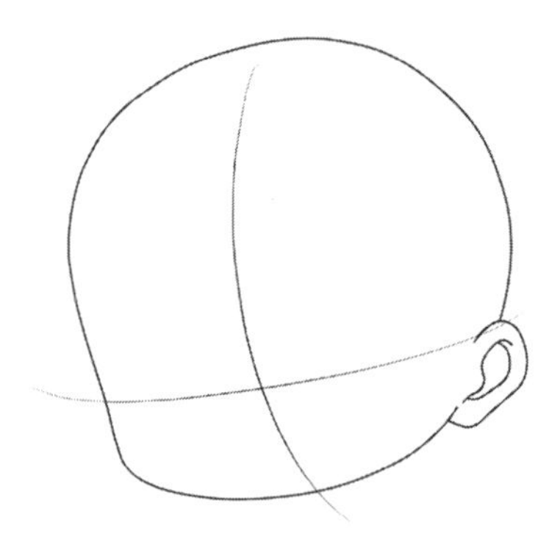

STEP 1 The faun starts out similar to the centaur, with a head that's round on the right side and flatter on the left. Place guidelines down the middle vertically and a little less than a third of the way up the head horizontally. Add a small ear that starts at the horizontal guideline on the right side of the head.

STEP 2 Draw a round eye on the right side of the head, a little above center from the guideline. Add a dark arch over the top.

STEP 3 Repeat on the other side. Add short, messy hair all around the head, going behind the ear.

STEP 4 Sketch in eyebrows and small triangles at the top of the head for horns. Draw a triangular tuft of fur under the head.

STEP 5 Start to draw the body by making two curves joined to the fur you just drew. Add a mouth by drawing a half circle below the eyes. Add segments to the horns.

STEP 6

Add a small triangular beard below the mouth, as well as short arms and hands. Make the left hand open, with palm facing back, and the right hand raised, with fingers closed. Draw oval-shaped ears on the sides of the head.

STEP 7

Draw a spear—a stick with a triangle on top—in the faun's right hand. Finish the body by rounding out the back and adding a curved line for the hip. Make these lines a little rough because this part of the body is fur.

STEP 8

Make the faun's legs with knees bent and curves at the end for the hooves. Erase the guidelines and add details to the eyes and blush on the cheeks. Add a line in the mouth for teeth.

Practice drawing the faun below!

Keep going from step 1.

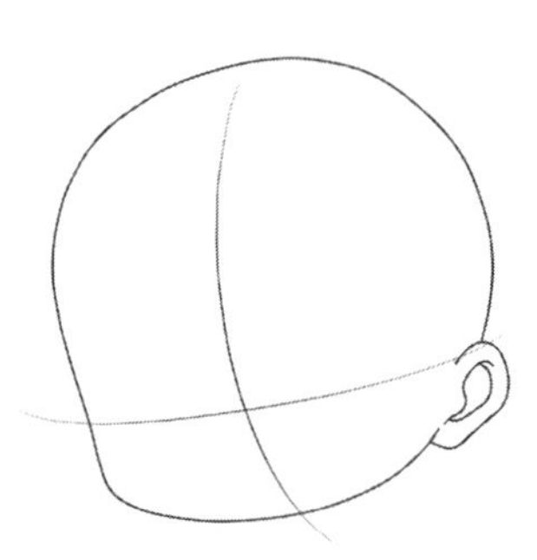

Try a few from scratch.

MINOTAUR

Many mythological human/animal combinations have the head of a person and the body of an animal, but the Minotaur is often shown with the head and often back legs/tail of a bull and the body of a person. Our version combines person and bull with a cute face with horns, human arms, and animal legs. Add a tail if you'd like to!

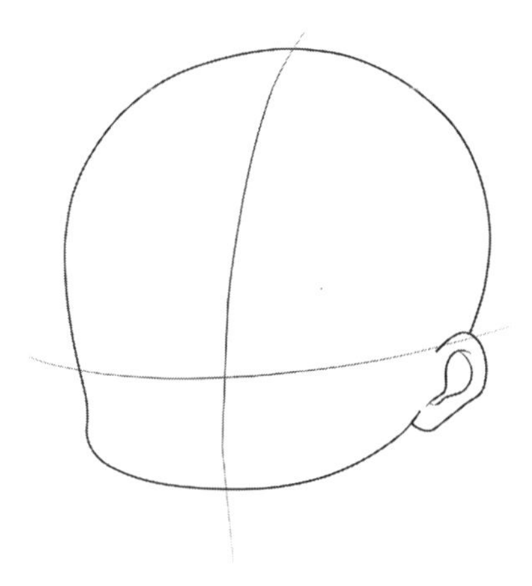

STEP 1 Draw a head that is round at the back with straighter sides. Make a guideline up the middle vertically and horizontally a little less than a third of the way from the bottom of the head. Add an ear on the right side that starts at the guideline (though it will be covered with hair if you want to skip it).

STEP 2 Place an eye on the right side of the head, centered on the horizontal line. Add a darker line across the top.

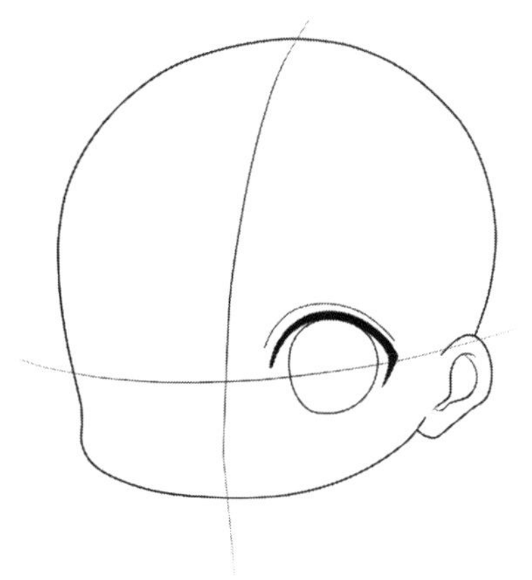

STEP 3

Make another eye, slightly smaller, on the left side. Add hair to the top of the head and a triangle on the right side behind the ear. Make a rough triangle of fur under the head.

STEP 4

Draw another triangular shape on the left side across from the one on the right. Sketch a jelly bean-shaped nose between and under the eyes. Add lines for the body and little marks for the Minotaur's muscles.

STEP 5

Add a ring to the nose. Add eyebrows and short arms. Make the right hand raised with fingers closed, and the left hand open, palm facing back.

STEP 6

Draw a rectangle of fur at the Minotaur's waist. Add curved triangle horns at the back sides of the head.

STEP 7

Add short lines for legs and give the Minotaur a spear, a stick with a spade shape on top.

STEP 8

Make rounded hooves with three toes at the end of each leg. Erase the guidelines and add details to the eyes.

Practice drawing the Minotaur below!

Keep going from step 1.

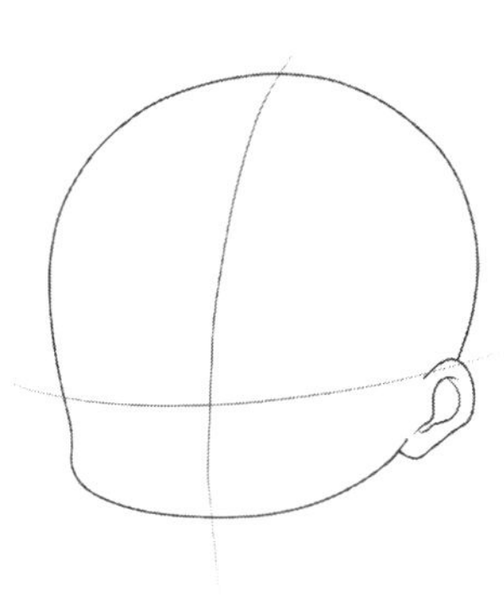

Try a few from scratch.

GRIFFIN

In mythology, a griffin is a creature with the head of an eagle and the body and tail of a lion. These animals are often shown with wings as well. If you want to add wings to yours, you can use a style similar to Pegasus found on page 152.

STEP 1

Start with a circle for the face, with the lower left bumped out a little for a cheek. Add guidelines centered vertically and horizontally.

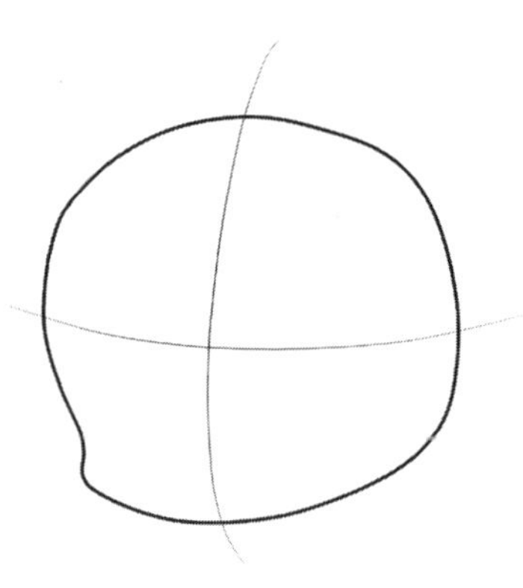

STEP 2

Draw in some eagle hair. Start with bangs going from the top left around the head to the bottom right, then add a swoop of spiky hair on top.

STEP 3

Add a large oval eye on the right side of the face, a little higher than center.

STEP 4

Repeat on the left side, then add a couple layers of feathers around the neckline.

STEP 5

Sketch in curves for the whites of the eyes and draw the body, which is a slightly curvy rectangle.

STEP 6

Add legs. This griffin will be in the sitting position, so draw the front legs stretched out and the back legs under the body. Give each paw three toes. Draw a mouth that is lemon shaped.

STEP 7

Next, draw a skinny tail in an S shape coming from the lower back. Tip the tail with a bit of fluff. Add a line to the mouth to make it more beak-like.

STEP 8

Erase your guidelines and add in details for the eyes and blush on the cheeks.

Practice drawing the griffin below!

Keep going from step 1.

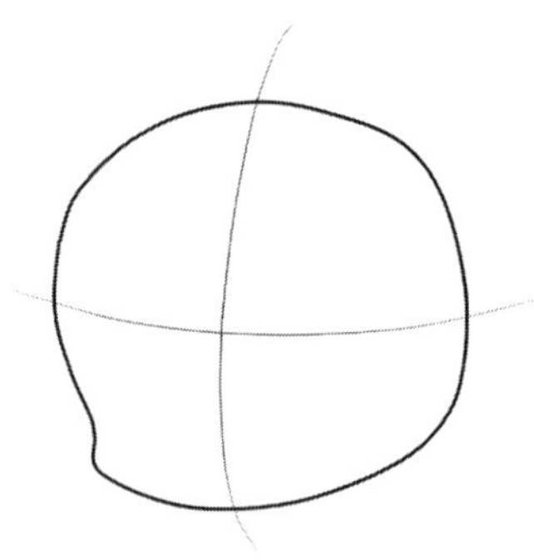

Try a few from scratch.

NINE-TAILED FOX

Found in the legends of Korea, China, and Japan, nine-tailed foxes are known for their ability to change shape, often to play tricks on people. But there's no trick behind this chibi version, which doesn't need to change shape to have a place in our hearts.

STEP 1 Sketch out a circle for the face. Add guidelines roughly in the center vertically and a little below center horizontally.

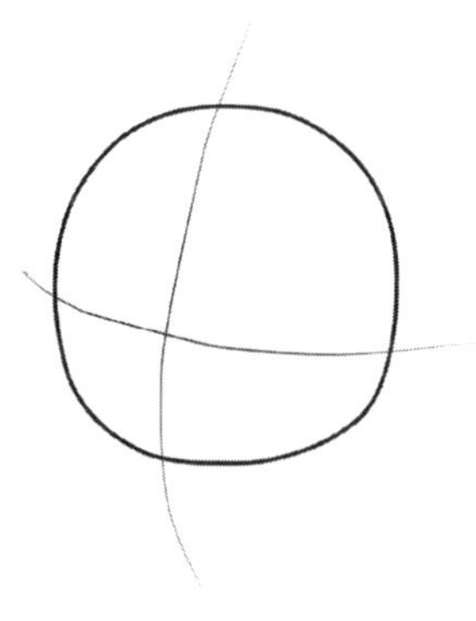

STEP 2 Add rough lines to the top of the face to make it furry, and draw furry, leaf-shaped fox ears on either side of the head.

STEP 3 Add a large circular eye on the horizontal guideline on the right side of the face.

STEP 4

Repeat on the left side, and draw an egg-shaped body connected to the head.

STEP 5

Add a fluffy, triangular bit of fur below the head.

STEP 6

Draw one leg at the front of the body, a curved line to represent another leg behind it, and the first fluffy tail crossing in front of the body.

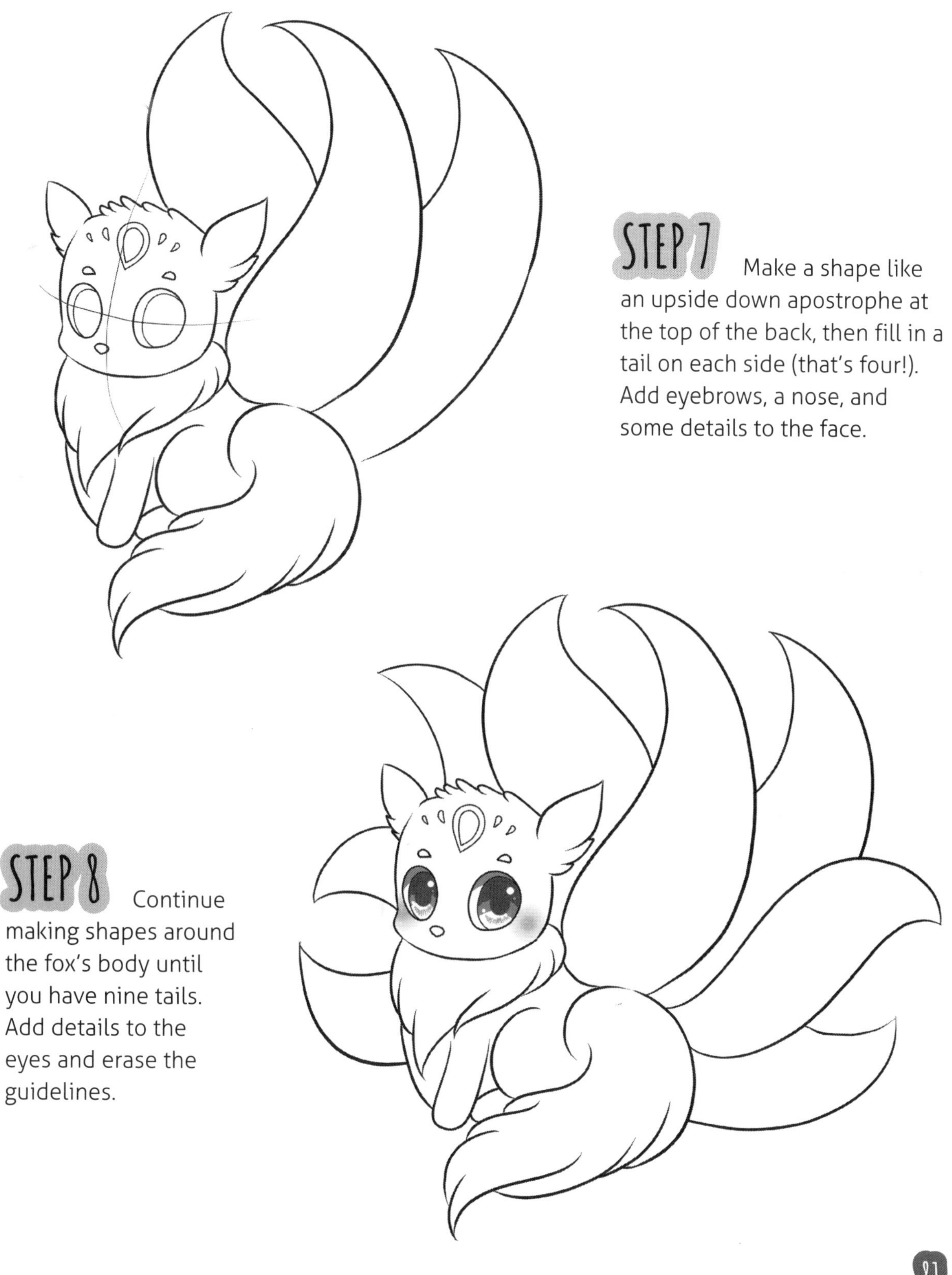

STEP 7

Make a shape like an upside down apostrophe at the top of the back, then fill in a tail on each side (that's four!). Add eyebrows, a nose, and some details to the face.

STEP 8

Continue making shapes around the fox's body until you have nine tails. Add details to the eyes and erase the guidelines.

Practice drawing the nine-tailed fox below!

Keep going from step 1.

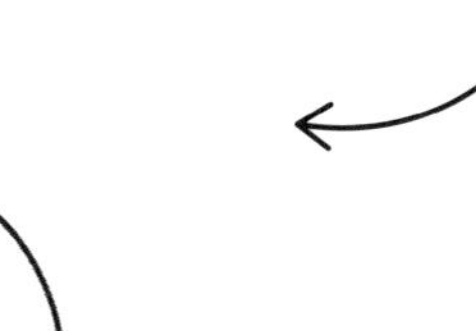

Try a few from scratch.

CERBERUS

Cerberus is known as the vicious three-headed dog that guards the gates of the underworld. But there's nothing scary about this version, except perhaps the amount of drool that will come from three dog heads covering you with kisses.

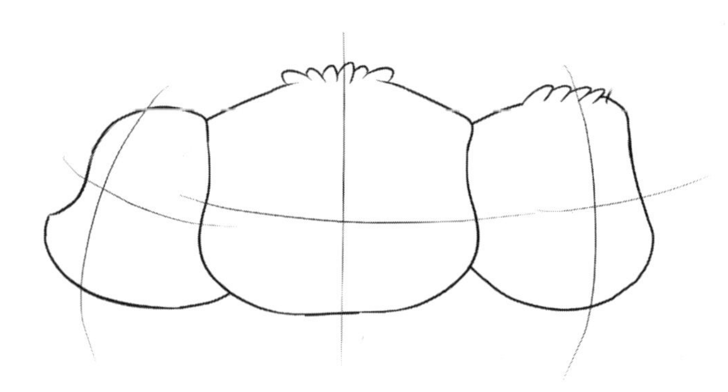

STEP 1 Cerberus has three heads, so let's start there. Draw the center head so it's facing forward and has a triangular top with a little hair at the center. The sides of the head should be mostly straight with a curved edge at the bottom. Draw a head on either side. In this example, the one on the right is looking more forward while the one on the left is looking to the side. Sketch some guidelines on each face as shown.

STEP 2 Add floppy ears: two to the one in the middle, one at the far right for the head on the right, and one at the far left for the head on the left.

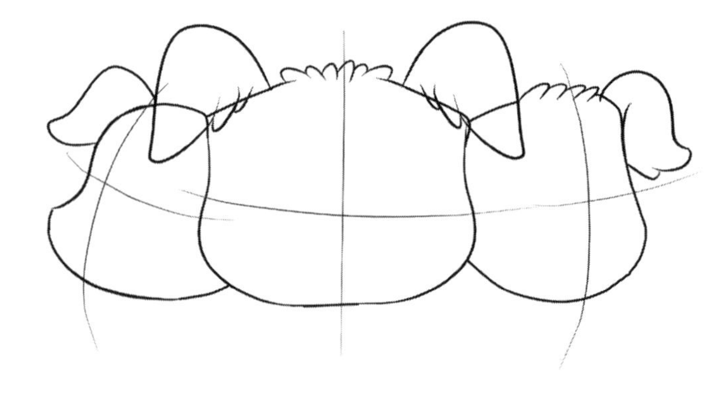

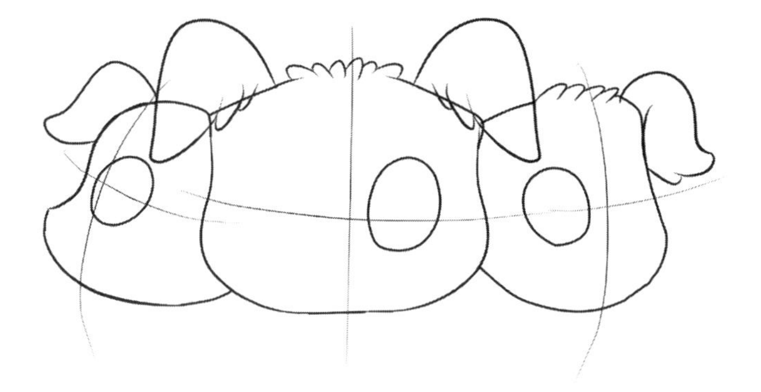

STEP 3

The eyes are large ovals that take up most of the center of each side of the face. Add one to each head.

STEP 4

Add a second whole eye to the center head and a partial eye on the right side of the right head. Draw in the white part of the left head's eye. Sketch in some scalloped lines to start to form the fluffy neck of the pup.

STEP 5

Draw lines for the body, making it the size you would make it for the center head only. Include a curve for the back of the body and the back foot. Draw in the white part of the remaining eyes.

STEP 6

Add small round noses to each face.

STEP 7

Place front legs and paws at the front of the body.

STEP 8

Finish with a small tail and mouths for all three heads, with half-ovals for sticking-out tongues on the center and right head. The center head gets two eyebrows, while the left head gets one. Add final details to the eyes and cheeks, and erase guidelines.

Practice drawing Cerberus below!

Keep going from step 1.

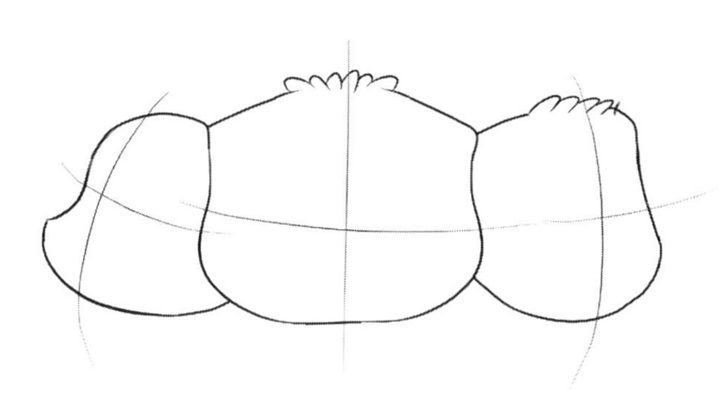

Try a few from scratch.

Yetis have a bad reputation for being rather scary loners, but perhaps this creature is misunderstood. Maybe they just need a hug? This fuzzy yeti is fun and fast to draw and looks a little like a sheep standing on two legs.

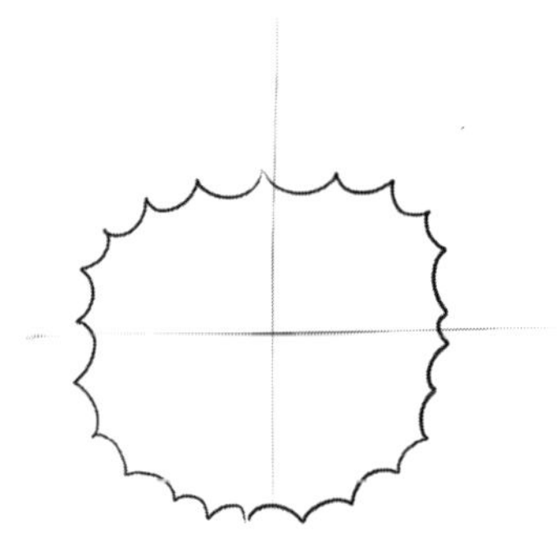

STEP 1 Begin the yeti's face with a scallop-edged circular shape.

STEP 2 Add a fuzzy gumdrop shape around the outside of the face, and a large oval eye on the right side of the face.

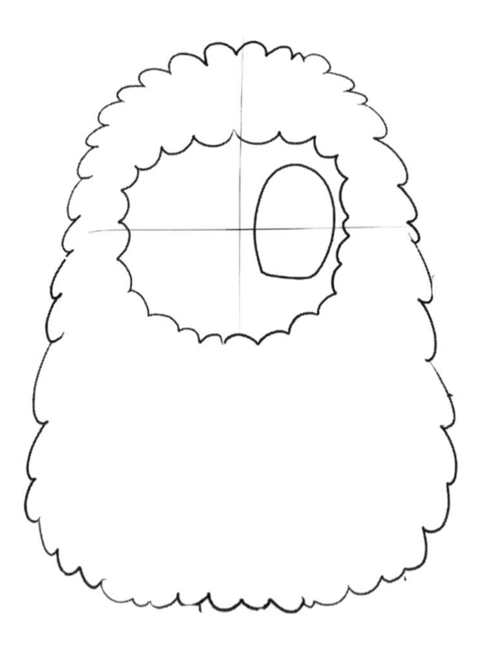

STEP 3

Repeat the eye on the left side, then add fuzzy little arms and a cone-shaped horn on the right side of the top of the head.

STEP 4

Make another horn on the left side, and add fuzzy little legs. Draw in the whites of the eyes.

STEP 5 Give your yeti hands by drawing little fingers at the ends of the arms. Add a semicircle for a nose between the eyes.

STEP 6 To make the mouth, create a larger semicircle below the nose.

STEP 7

Add two little teeth inside the mouth and feet at the ends of the legs.

STEP 8

Draw in the eye details and a little blush on the cheeks—it's cold out there!

Practice drawing the yeti below!

Keep going from step 1.

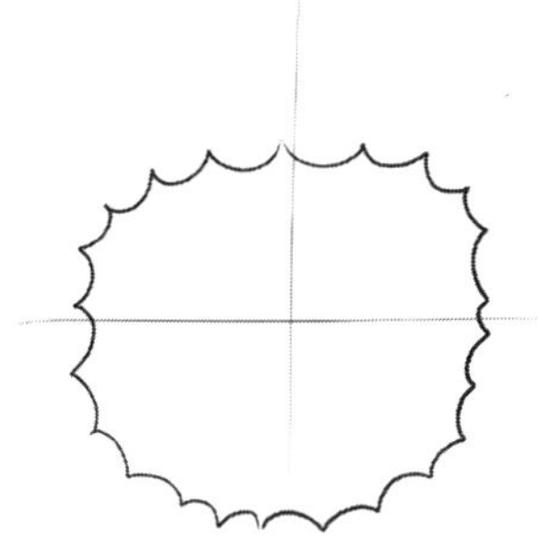

Try a few from scratch.

GODZILLA

Godzilla is known as a gigantic, destructive sea monster, but this chibi version won't destroy anything but our hearts. I don't know what's cuter—the giant eyes or the tiny teeth! Or maybe it's those itty-bitty arms.

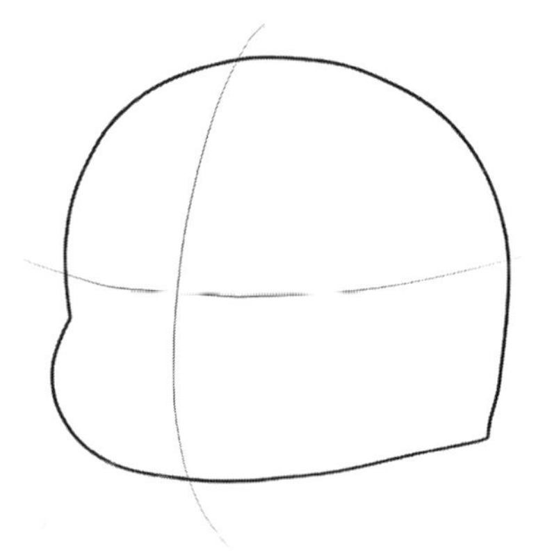

STEP 1 Draw the head a bit like a slightly smooshed heart on its side. Create a round top that comes to a point like the bottom of a heart at the bottom right. Make the bottom of the face almost straight, with a little curve at the bottom left. Center the horizontal guideline on the face, and the vertical one closer to the left side.

STEP 2 Make a large shape like a slightly flattened oval for the right eye. It should be a little higher than centered on the guideline. Start to form the body with a curved line at the front and a slightly diagonal line at the back.

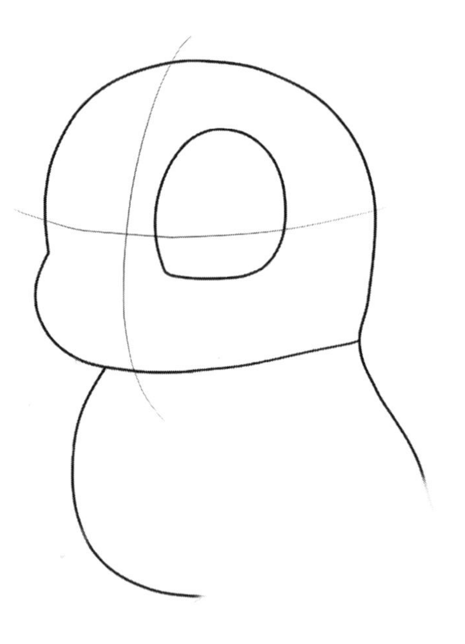

STEP 3 Lengthen the line at the back slightly and add an oval eye on the left side that runs into the side of the face. Draw a short arm with three little claws up against the body on the left side.

STEP 4 Sketch in the whites of the eyes. Add a curved line around the center of the body for the back leg. Draw a second arm on the right side, stretching out in front of the body.

STEP 5

Add eyebrows over the eyes. The left-side brow can go a little off the face so it looks like it's standing up. Add a three-toed foot on the left side.

STEP 6

Continue the leg line into another foot and the back of the body into the tail. Add an open mouth that looks like a jellybean on its side.

STEP 7

Sketch in nostrils above the mouth, near the vertical guideline. Draw triangular spikes from the top of the head down to where the head joins the body. Add horizontal lines across the belly.

STEP 8

Continue the spikes down the tail. Add a row of teeth to the mouth. Erase the guidelines and add details to the eyes and a bit of blush to the right cheek.

Practice drawing Godzilla below!

Keep going from step 1.

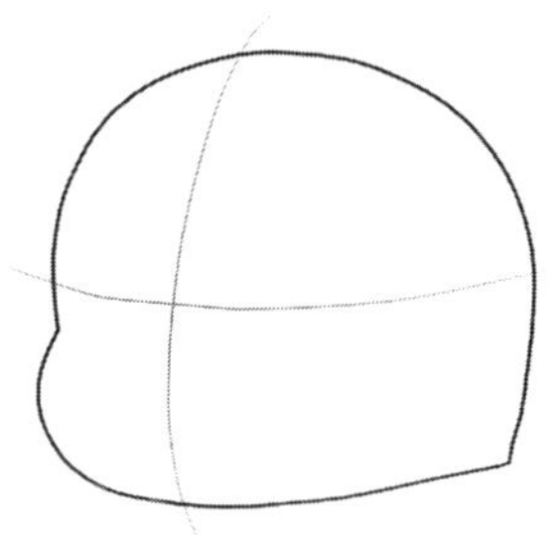

Try a few from scratch.

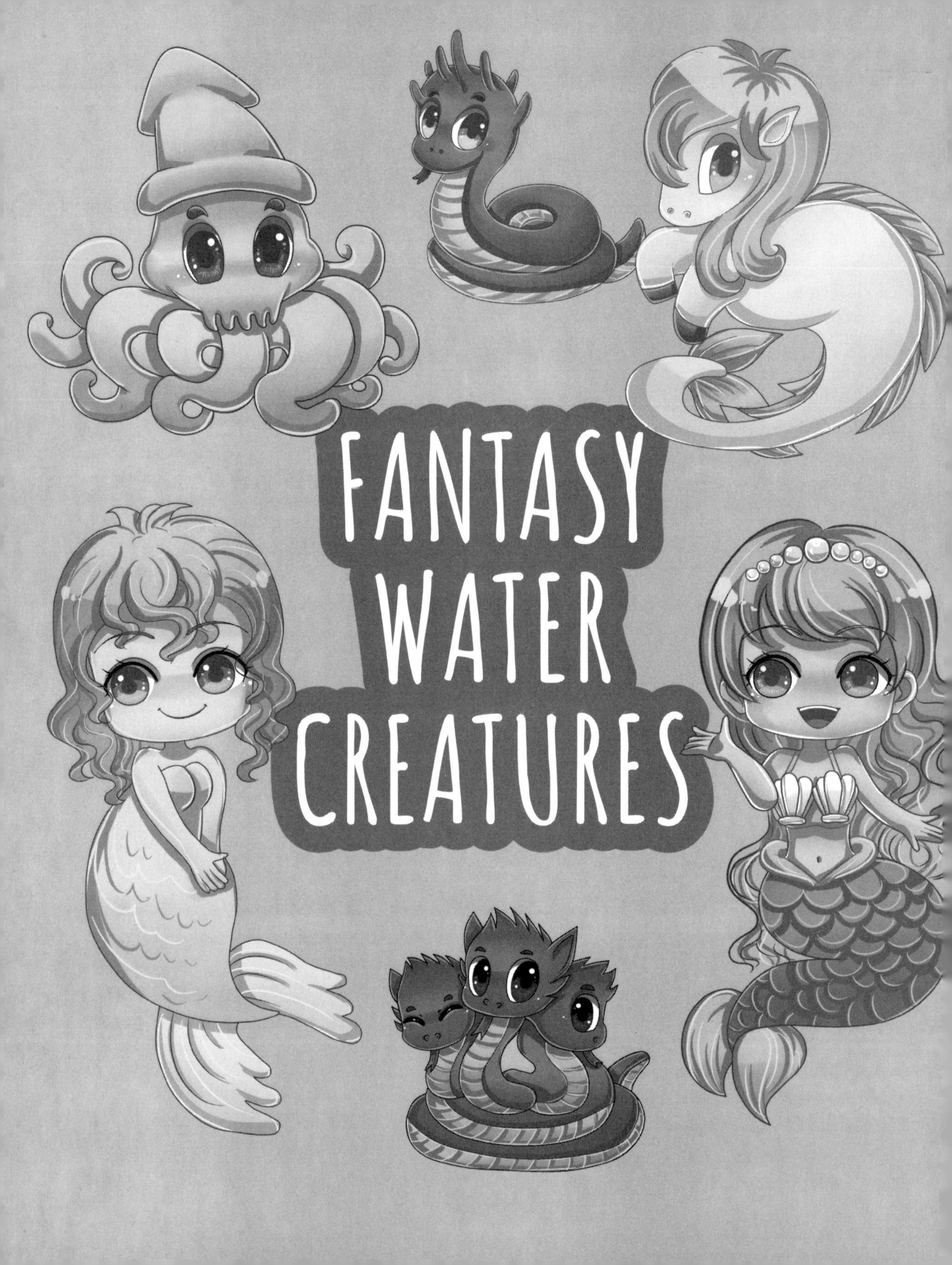
FANTASY
WATER
CREATURES

MERMAID

Mermaids are a lot of fun to draw because you can use whatever colors you like to give them a different look. Use your favorite colors, the colors of your school, or those of your favorite sports team. The sky is the limit!

STEP 1 Sketch out the mermaid's head. The top of the head should be round, while the sides should be straight and end with a blocky jawline. Add round ears very low on the sides of the face, and sketch in guidelines straight up the center vertically and around the top of the ears horizontally.

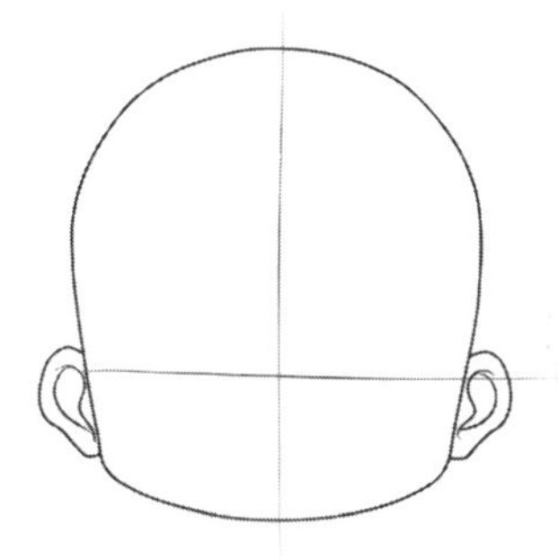

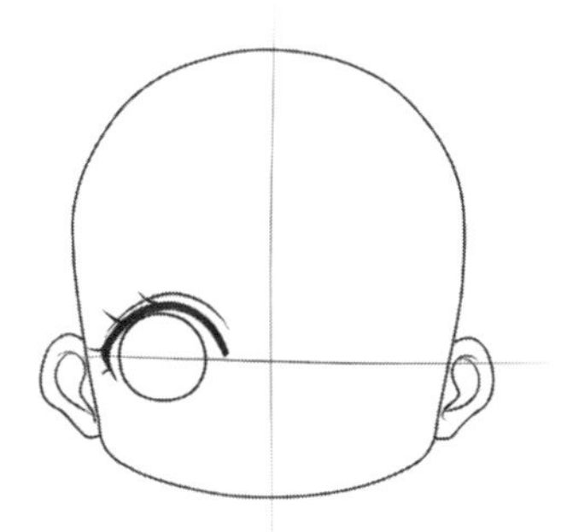

STEP 2 Add an eye on the left side of the face, centered on the horizontal guideline. Don't forget the eyelashes!

STEP 3 Start to draw in hair. This mermaid has sweeping long bangs that go down almost to the eyes and wavy curls on the right side of the face.

STEP 4

Draw the eye on the right side of the face. Begin to sketch in the body, with a thin neck and shoulders, shell bra, narrow waist, and curving lines around the waist to make the top of the tail. The body should be narrower than the head.

STEP 5

Include short little arms. The one on the left is raised, with palm facing up and fingers spread. The right arm points down between the body and the hair, with fingers following the line of the hand. Add in eyebrows under the bangs and a headband of pearls along the hairline behind the bangs.

STEP 6

Let's give our mermaid a tail! Curve the tail out like a big apostrophe on its side, with the point being the end of the tail on the left side. Draw an open mouth like a half circle below and in between the eyes.

STEP 7

Give the tail two leaf-shaped fins at the end.

STEP 8 Add details to the eyes, erase the guidelines, add half-circle shapes for scales on the tail, and add a little more hair flowing down almost to the end of the mermaid's tail on the left side.

Practice drawing the mermaid below!

Keep going from step 1.

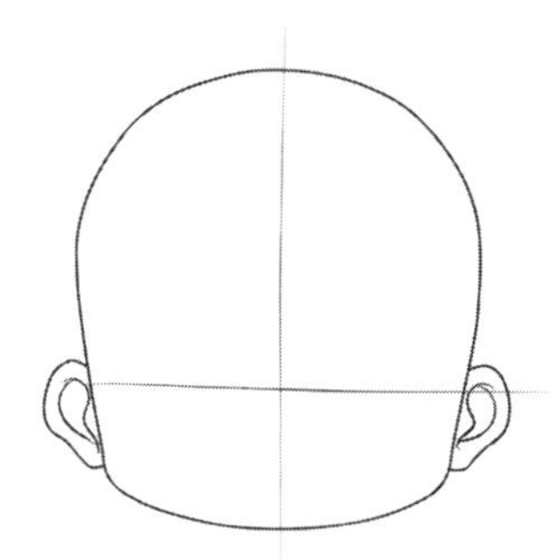

Try a few from scratch.

SELKIE

A selkie looks somewhat like a mermaid, but instead of being part fish, a selkie is part seal. It's said a selkie can turn into a seal, then shed its skin and become a human. This version is more of a half person, half seal, but it's definitely 100 percent cute.

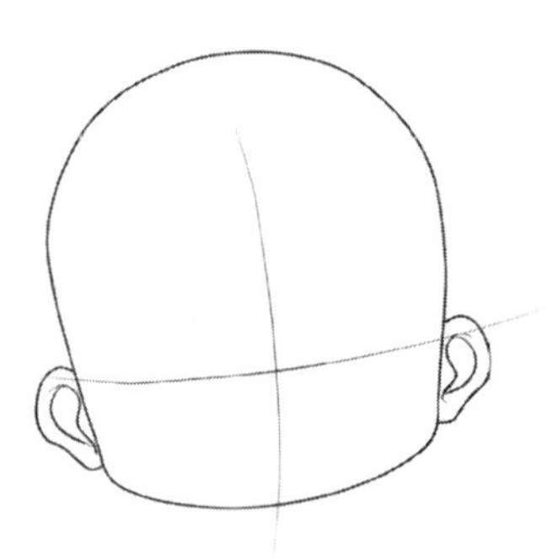

STEP 1 Start by drawing a head that is round at the top, straight at the sides, and slightly curved along the bottom. Add a vertical guideline straight through the middle and a horizontal line about a third of the way from the bottom of the head. If you'd like, you can add small half-circle ears below the horizontal line, but these will be covered by hair.

STEP 2 Add an eye on the left side of the face, centered on the horizontal line. Make a darker line at the top of the eye, following its shape.

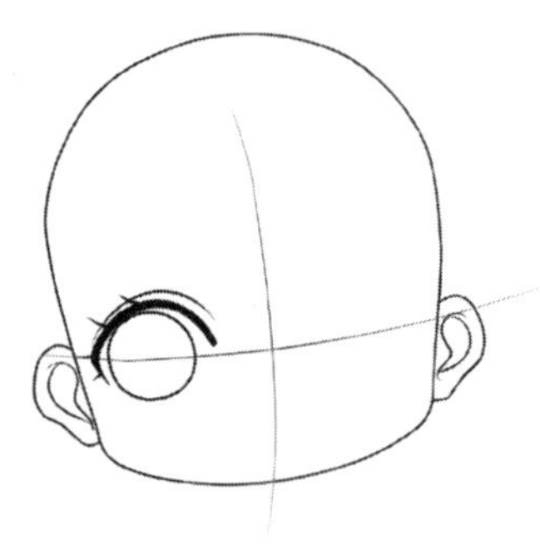

STEP 3

Make another eye on the right side, then add a short neck, shoulders, and the top of her bodice.

STEP 4

Sketch long curved eyebrows over the eyes, roughly in the center of the head vertically. Our selkie has long, thin arms that are crossed in front of the body. Draw the fingers of the left hand. Add a curved line for a smile below and between the eyes.

STEP 5

Draw the selkie's body, which is one long curve on the left side and a shorter, backwards S shape on the right, coming to a point for the tail.

STEP 6

Add wavy bangs and shoulder-length hair, with just a little tuft sticking up at the top for extra cuteness.

STEP 7

Draw a feathery looking flipper at the bottom on the left side of the tail.

STEP 8

Make another flipper on the right side. Erase the guidelines and add details to the eyes.

Practice drawing the selkie below!

Keep going from step 1.

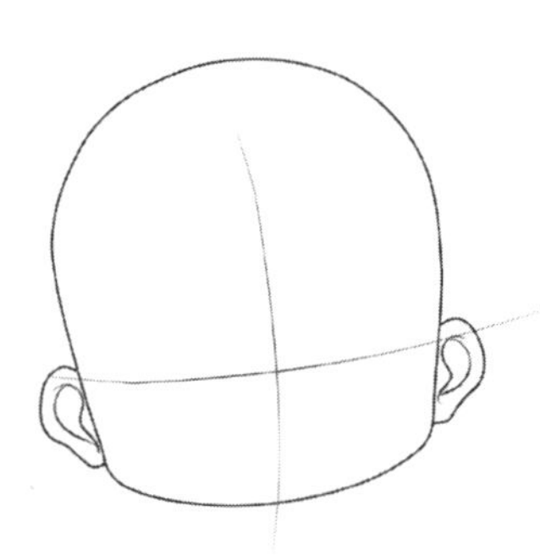

Try a few from scratch.

KELPIE

The kelpie is a shape-shifting water spirit found in Scottish folklore. This version looks like a pony with the tail of a sea serpent. Give yours a standard horse color or color it in pastels.

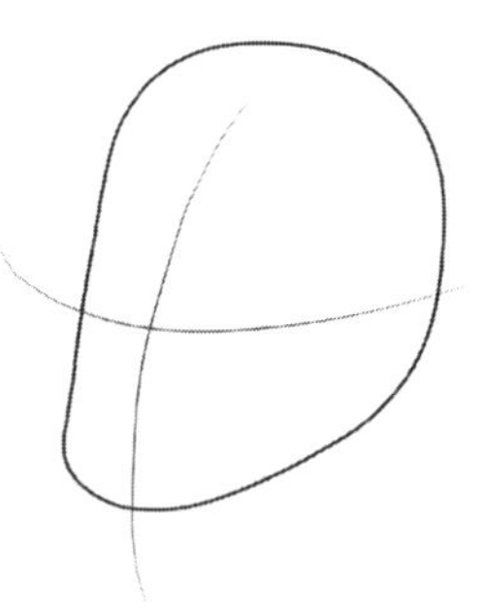

STEP 1 The face of the kelpie looks like a horse's snout. Start the circle with a straight line on the left side, a curve at the top, and continue until it squares off a bit at the bottom. The vertical guideline bisects the muzzle, and the horizontal one is a little lower than the center of the head.

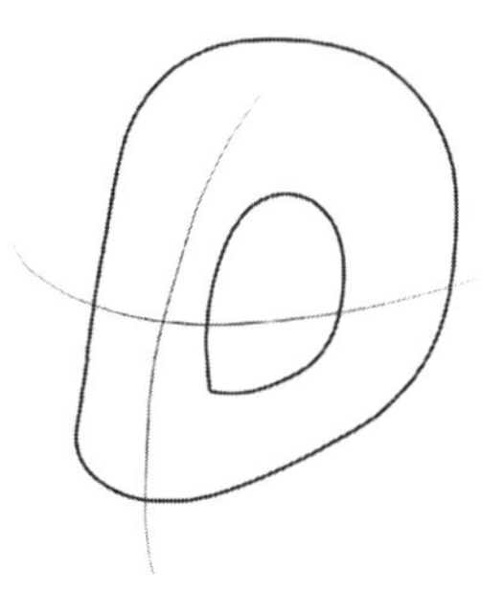

STEP 2 Draw a large almond-shaped eye on the right side of the face.

STEP 3 Add a curve inside the eye for the white, and a little pointed ear near the top of the right side of the head.

STEP 4 Sketch in the hair. Have the bangs flow to the left over where the eye would be on that side, and draw longer hair cascading down the right side behind the head. Add circles low on the muzzle for the nostrils.

STEP 5 Form the body with a large oval connected to the bottom right of the head.

STEP 6 Make two little legs, with hooves at the front of the body.

STEP 7 Starting at the back of body, draw a curving tail that makes the whole body look like an apostrophe.

STEP 8 Add feathery accents along the back of the body and at the tip of the tail. Erase the guidelines and add details to the eye and blush to the cheek.

Practice drawing the kelpie below!

Keep going from step 1.

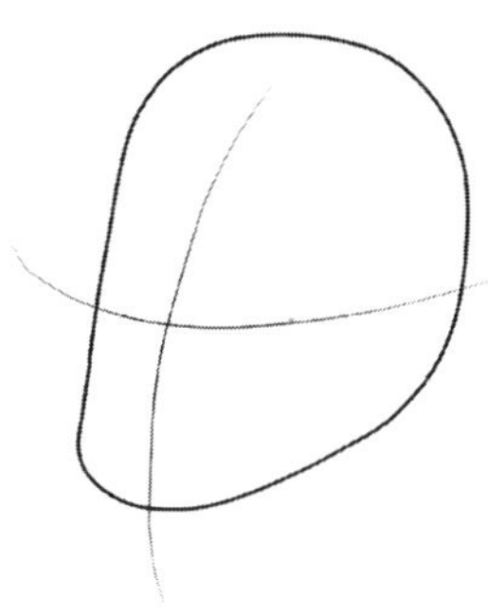

Try a few from scratch.

BASILISK

The legendary basilisk is a serpent king that can cause death at a glance, but the only danger in looking at this sweet snake is cuteness overload. The spikes on its head and the little forked tongue give this drawing lots of personality.

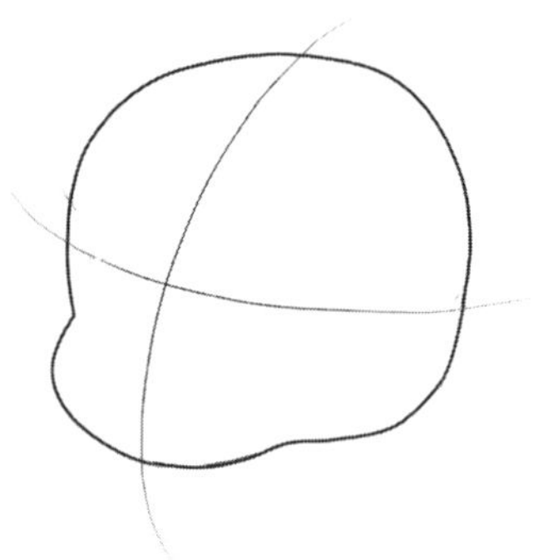

STEP 1 Start with the head, which is mostly round but with a part jutting out that looks like a chin. (It's actually the basilisk's mouth.) Add guidelines to segment the face into quarters.

STEP 2 Sketch in a large oval eye on the right side of the face. Add spikes of various heights on top of the head. This example shows seven, but you can include as many as you want.

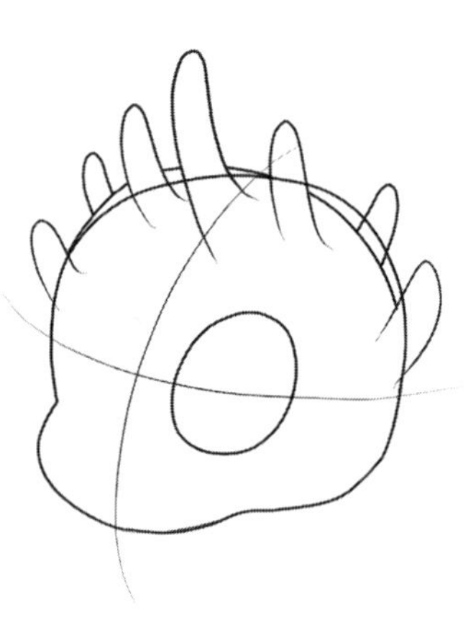

STEP 3

Draw a second eye on the left side of the face. Begin shaping the snake's body with two lines that begin at the bottom of the face and slowly spiral back to begin to form the tail.

STEP 4

Add another line below the first two to indicate another layer of the serpent's body, then draw the tip of the tail. Draw in the white part of the eyes.

STEP 5 Sketch in lines along the body and tail to set off the center part of the body.

STEP 6 Include horizontal lines across the center section of the "chest" of the basilisk.

STEP 7 Continue adding horizontal lines on the lower part of the body and the tip of the tail. Draw in eyebrows over the eyes and breathing holes between and below the eyes.

STEP 8 Erase the guidelines, fill in the details of the eyes, and add a little blush to the cheeks. Don't forget to add a tiny forked tongue!

Practice drawing the basilisk below!

Keep going from step 1.

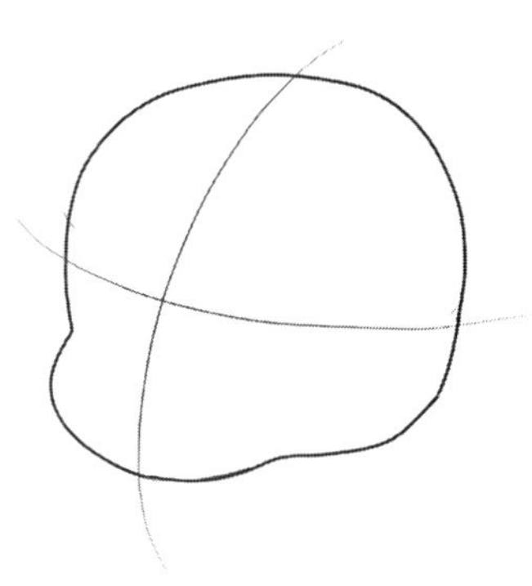

Try a few from scratch.

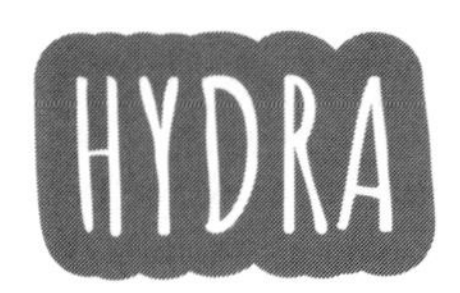

HYDRA

Like Cerberus, shown on page 84, this hydra has three adorable heads. In mythology, hydras have up to nine heads, so you can keep adding heads and snaky bodies as shown if you want your creature to have more.

STEP 1 Start by thinking about head placement. In this example, the heads all overlap a little, and the right head is turned to the right, while the left and center heads are more straight on. First, draw the center head, which is wider than the others. Draw the right head in more of an oval shape and the left head more like a square with rounded corners. Add guidelines in the center horizontally and vertically on the front and left heads, and on the right head such that the guidelines meet at the right side of the part of the face that is shown.

STEP 2 Give the center head two petal-shaped ears, and the head on the left, one. Give all three spiky hair on top.

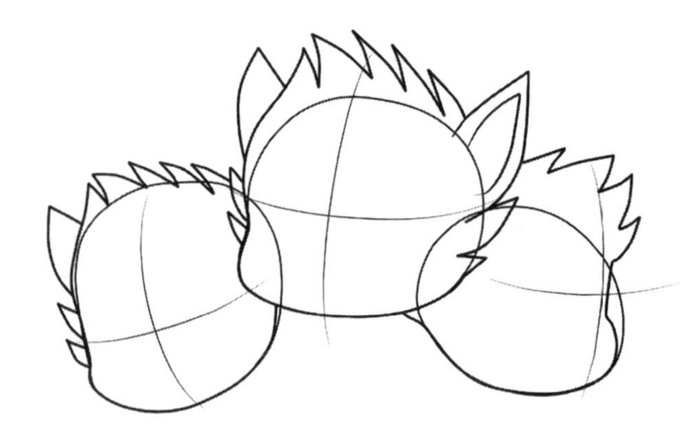

STEP 3 Now for the eyes. For the center head, add large oval eyes centered on the face. Give the right head one full eye, with just a tiny bit of the second eye visible. The left head has squinting eyes; you can draw those like little arches on the horizontal guideline.

STEP 4 Sketch the whites of the eyes, and add tiny white dots to the eyes that are squinting. Add eyebrows just over the eyes on the left head, and nostrils on each side of the vertical guideline on the left and center face. For the face on the right, draw one nostril to the left of the vertical guideline.

STEP 5 Draw eyebrows on the other heads and little forked tongues below the nostrils on each face. Give each head a little serpent body.

STEP 6 Add lines to the bodies to mark off the center part of the body.

STEP 7 Continue the curve from the right-hand side of the body and make two loops of snake tail underneath the three heads. Don't forget the end of the tail peeking up on the right side.

STEP 8 Add horizontal lines in the center section of the bodies and along the bottom of the tail parts you just drew. Erase the guidelines and add details to the eyes and blush to the cheeks.

Practice drawing the hydra below!

Keep going from step 1.

Try a few from scratch.

KRAKEN

When it comes to legendary sea monsters, there's none bigger or badder than the kraken. This ancient beast was said to be able to demolish whole ships with its giant tentacles. Our version is a little tamer and a lot of fun to draw.

STEP 1 Draw the beginning of the kraken's head like a big potato on its side. Sketch in guidelines across the center horizontally and vertically.

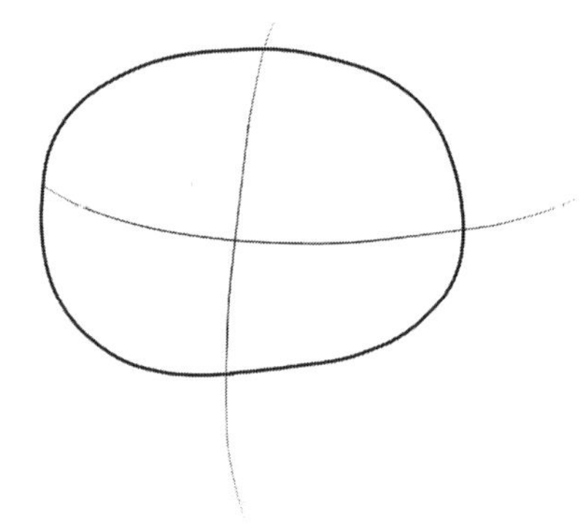

STEP 2 At the center bottom of the head, draw short wavy lines for the mouth tentacles. Make little curves on the sides of the face below the horizontal guideline to give the kraken cheeks.

STEP 3 Add a large oval on the right side of the face for one eye.

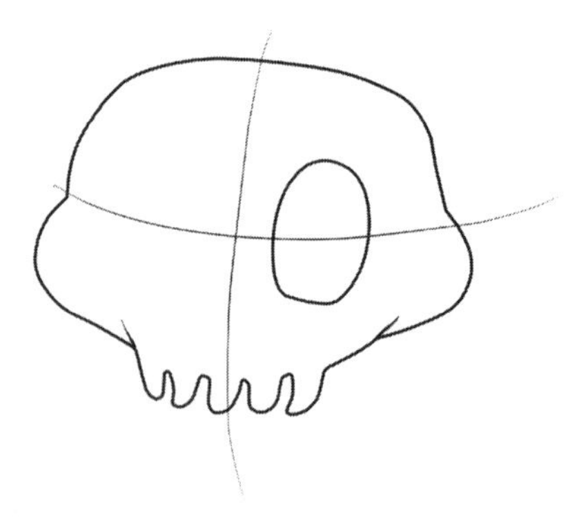

STEP 4 Draw the second eye and the squid-like appendage at the top of the kraken's head. It looks like a puffy arrow.

STEP 5 Add eyebrows and a curve inside the eyes for the whites. Make one tentacle curving down and around from the center of the head.

STEP 6

Now, draw another tentacle to the left of the first. The bottoms of these are curved almost like little feet.

STEP 7

Keep adding tentacles around the bottom. At the end of this step, you should have five.

STEP 8 Add more tentacles until the body is nicely filled in. If your sea monster is octopus based, you should have eight, but add as many as looks good to you. Include details in the eyes and a bit of blush on the cheeks. Erase your guidelines.

Practice drawing the kraken below!

Keep going from step 1.

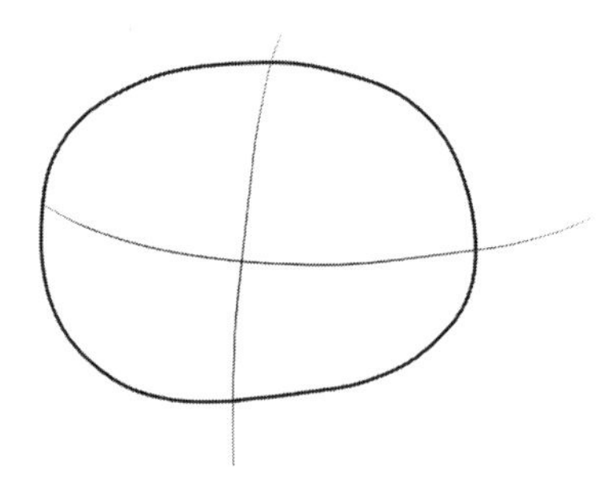

Try a few from scratch.

FANTASY
WINGED
CREATURES

The phoenix is famously a bird of reinvention, bursting into flames only to emerge from the ashes as a new creature. This phoenix is drawn with flame-like feathers. Color yours in the shades of fire or use any other colors you like.

STEP 1 Draw a small circle for the head. Lightly sketch in horizontal and vertical guidelines.

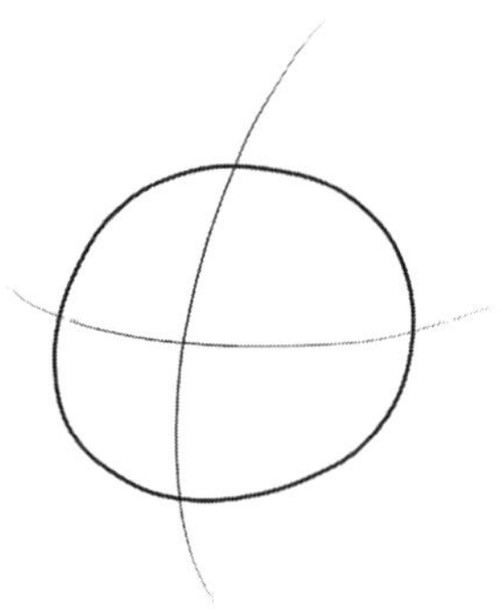

STEP 2 Draw spiky, flame-like feathers around the sides of the face, with the longest feather at the top and shorter feathers on each side.

STEP 3 Sketch in a large oval eye on the right side of the face, centered on the horizontal guideline and close to the center of the face. Add a feathery oval below the head for the bird's body.

STEP 4 Make another eye on the left side of the face and draw in longer, pointier feathers on the left side of the body for the wing.

STEP 5 Draw another wing on the right side of the body. Sketch arches at the top of the eye circles for the whites.

STEP 6 Add short eyebrows above each eye and short, three-toed legs at the center bottom of the body.

STEP 7 This phoenix has a fluffy tail shaped like an upside-down flame. draw it starting behind the right wing and going around to the left foot. Don't forget the cute little curl at the end! Add a rounded triangle for the beak.

STEP 8 Erase the guidelines and add in details for the eyes, a bit of blush, and little horns that curl in toward the top of the head.

Practice drawing the phoenix below!

Keep going from step 1.

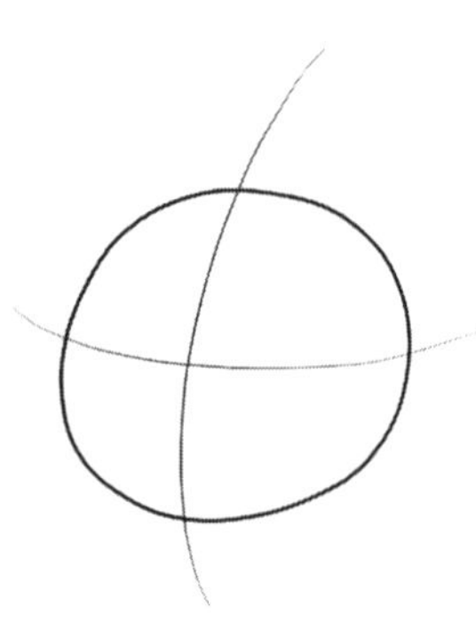

Try a few from scratch.

SPHINX

The sphinx is known for being a puzzling trickster, but there's no real trick to drawing one. The combination of a human head, lion's body, and wings includes lots of parts we've used in other drawings. There's certainly no riddle to this creature's cuteness.

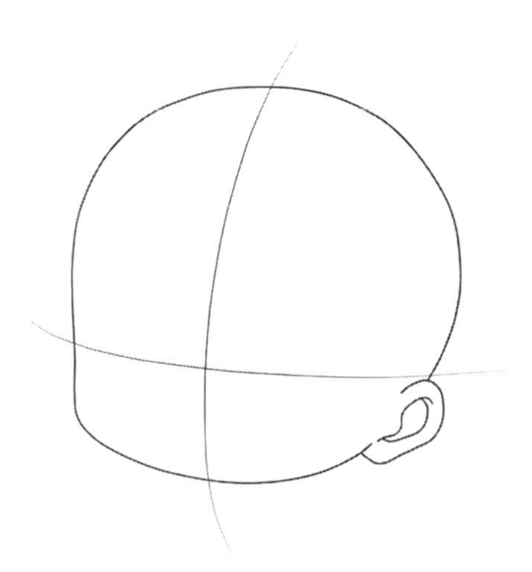

STEP 1 Start with the human head. The front of the face should be blocky, with a curve at the back of the head. Draw the vertical guideline so that it divides the face in half, and the horizontal one along the bottom third of the face. Draw a small ear on the right side, under the guideline.

STEP 2 Add a round eye on the horizontal line on the right side, and a thick arch over it to highlight the eyelid.

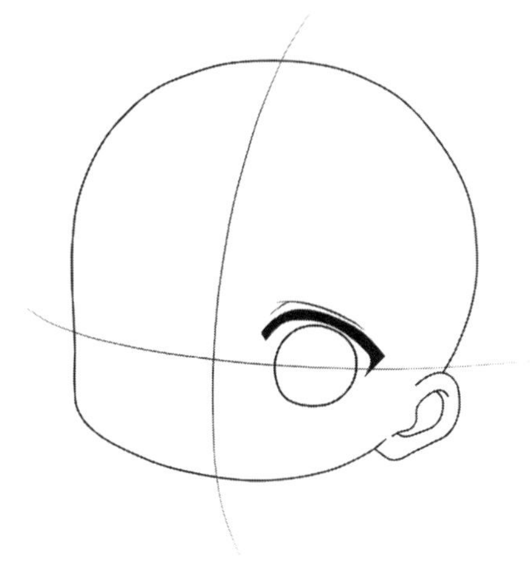

STEP 3 Repeat on the left side, then draw cascading hair and wavy bangs.

STEP 4 Draw in eyebrows that repeat the arch of the eye above each eye, and a little tuft of fur below the center of the face.

STEP 5 Make a half circle for a mouth centered below the eyes, and add a rough oval attached to the tuft of fur and going to the right for the body.

STEP 6

Give your sphinx four standing legs and feet with three toes each, though you can't see all the toes as drawn.

STEP 7

Add pointy ears on the sides of the head and a short tail with a tuft of fur at the end.

STEP 8 Erase the guidelines and add details to the eyes. Place a star in the sphinx's hair and give it wings along the back of the body.

Practice drawing the sphinx below!

Keep going from step 1.

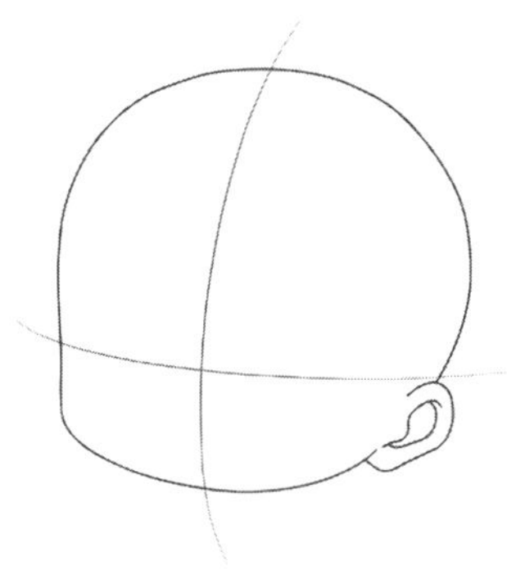

Try a few from scratch.

A chimera is a creature with a lot going on. There are different versions in mythology, but common components are a lion with an extra goat's head, eagle's wings coming out of its back, and a serpent for a tail. How can that possibly be cute? Let's find out!

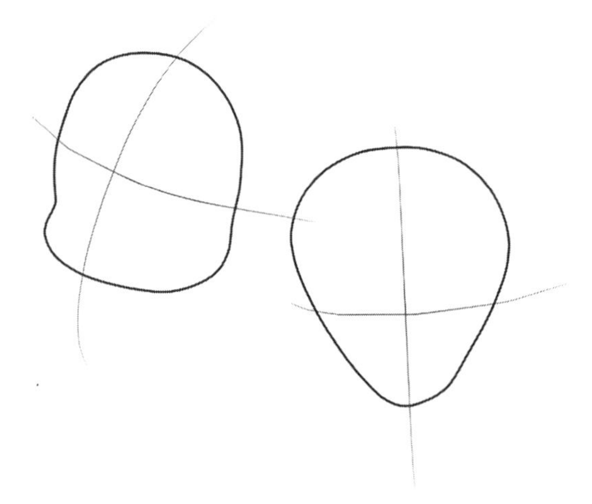

STEP 1 Start with the two heads. Shape the goat's head like a guitar pick (round at the top, with a rounded triangle shape at the bottom) and have it face forward. To the left of the goat's head, shape the lion's head almost like a square with curved edges, turned slightly to the side. Sketch in guidelines to divide each face in half vertically. The horizontal guideline on the goat's head should be about two-thirds down rather than centered.

STEP 2 Add the goat's ears near the top of each side of the head. The goat will be squinting, so draw a slanted eyebrow shape on the right horizontal guideline for its eye, with a small white dot in the center. Sketch a large oval-shaped eye on the right side of the lion's head and add hair all the way around the face.

STEP 3 Repeat the eyes on the other sides of the faces (the lion's second eye should be a little smaller). Draw a long oval for the body.

STEP 4 Give the goat tiny eyebrows and horns on the top of the head. Make a curve under the goat's head for the leg joint. Sketch in the beginnings of three legs. Add whites in the lion's eyes.

STEP 5

Add some feathered eagle's wings. Draw a nose on each face, and add three-toed paws to the end of each leg.

STEP 6

Make the chimera's tail an S-shaped snake with a round head at the end.

STEP 7

Give each face a mouth—a half circle for the lion and two little curves for the goat—and begin to sketch eyes for the serpent. Add more wings if desired.

STEP 8

Add details to the eyes of the lion and serpent, as well as a forked tongue for the snake and a little beard for the goat. Add horizontal lines to the goat's horns.

Practice drawing the chimera below!

Keep going from step 1.

Try a few from scratch.

PEGASUS

Pegasus is a unicorn with a major glow up: he has wings! This design is similar to the unicorn on page 49, but the creatures face different directions, so it's easy to combine them in a larger drawing, or make more than one unicorn or Pegasus facing both directions.

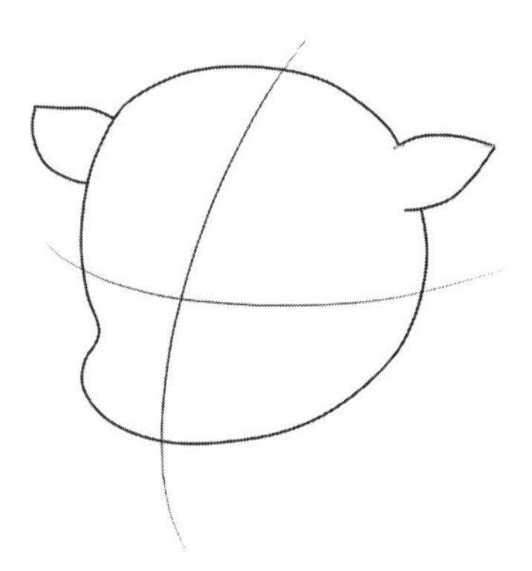

STEP 1 Start with a head that's mostly a circle, with a little piece bumped out at the bottom left for the nose. Add triangular ears that point straight out at the sides near the top, and sketch out guidelines through the center vertically and just above the nose horizontally.

STEP 2 Add a large oval eye on the right side of the face and a skinny oval on its side for the body.

STEP 3

Draw a second eye on the left side of the face. Add a line following the line of the right ear, just inside the original line. Begin to flesh out the body by making the back and bottom parts of the body straighter.

STEP 4

Give your Pegasus legs. In this example, the two in the front are aligned, while one leg is behind the other in the back, drawn as if the creature were walking. Add arcs to the inside of the left side of each eye to make the whites. Place a swirl of hair on top of its head.

STEP 5

Add lines a short distance up from the bottom of each foot to make the hooves. Add a cascade of hair from the swirl you started with that goes behind the head and over the shoulder. Add circles for the nostrils on either side of the vertical guideline, beneath the eyes.

STEP 6

Now, it's time to turn this horse into Pegasus. Draw a wing made of four segments that sits behind the hair on its back.

STEP 7

Sketch in a swoop of a tail below the wing.

STEP 8

Add details to the eyes, extra lines in the hair and tail to make them look wavy, and a little blush on the cheeks.

Practice drawing Pegasus below!

Keep going from step 1.

Try a few from scratch.

DRAGON

When you think of mythical creatures, the dragon is likely one of the first to come to mind. This one looks like it's more likely to be protecting a hoard of yarn balls rather than gold and treasure, but don't let the sweet exterior fool you. There's still fire in this dragon's blood!

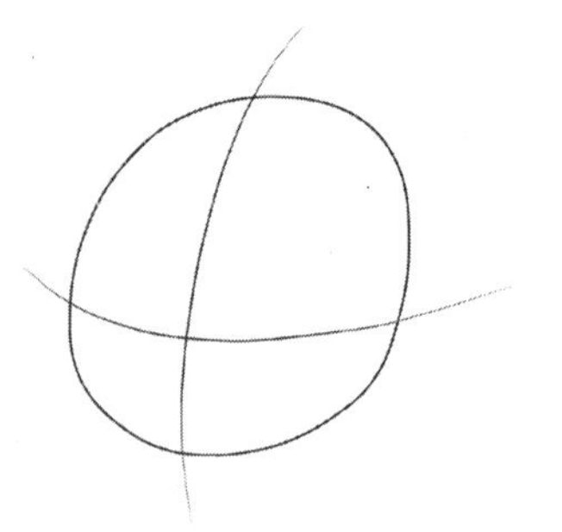

STEP 1 Start with a circle. Add light guidelines through the center of the circle vertically and slightly lower than the center horizontally.

STEP 2 Add curved horns on each side of the top of the head. Add tufts of hair between the horns and on the sides of the face.

STEP 3 Draw a large oval for the body, starting at the right side of the head and going around to the lower left side of the face. Draw a large circle centered on the right side of the horizontal guideline for the eye. Sketch a small crescent shape at the top of the eye. Add small horns with horizontal lines making a little triangle at the top and pointing inward on top of the head.

STEP 4 Add a smaller circle on the left side for the left eye and a crescent shape above as with the other eye. Draw short eyebrows over the eyes. Extend the curve of the back of the oval below the body to make a curving tail that points back toward the body. Add a curved line on the body intersecting the end of the tail, and two diagonal, parallel lines at the front for the leg.

STEP 5 Draw a small nose on the vertical guideline under the eyes. Add wing shapes to each side of the head and claws on the front foot. Make a flame-shaped tuft of fur at the end of the tail. Add claws under the tail to indicate another foot.

STEP 6 Add a smaller outline of the end of the tail shape inside the original tail lines.

STEP 7 Follow the shape of the left wing to separate it into four segments.

STEP 8 Repeat on the right wing. Add pupils and eye shine to the eyes. Carefully erase guidelines.

Practice drawing the dragon below!

Keep going from step 1.

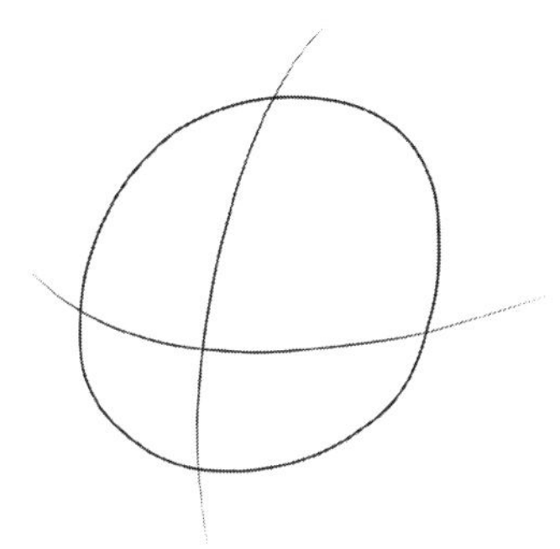

Try a few from scratch.

PERYTON

Have you heard of a peryton? This mythical creature is a combination of a stag and a bird, and it was said to live in Atlantis. Wherever it is from, this chibi version sure is sweet.

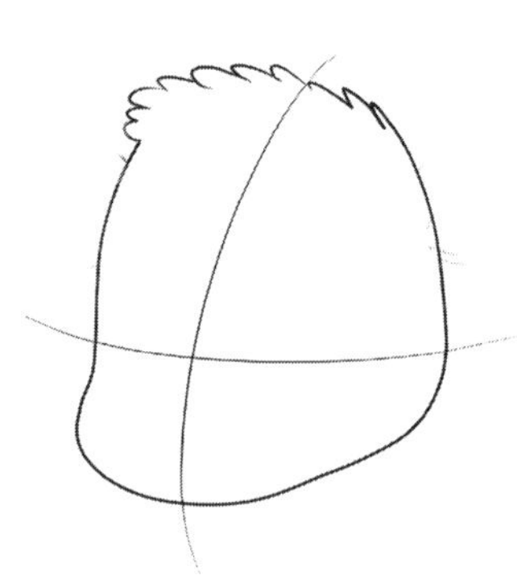

STEP 1 Start with the peryton's head—curved at the top and bottom, with straighter lines on the sides. Add a little fuzzy hair at the top and a guideline up and down the middle, with the horizontal line about a third of the way up the face.

STEP 2 Draw large almond-shaped eyes that cover most of the bottom part of the face. Sketch eyebrows and the whites of the eyes as well.

STEP 3 Add ears that stick out from the top of the head at the sides, and a little oval nose below and between the eyes.

STEP 4 Make the body a shape that looks like a heart with the bottom cut off.

STEP 5 Sketch in feathery wings at the top and toward the back of the body.

STEP 6 Draw four little legs and curves on the body for the leg joints.

STEP 7

Add antlers and hooves.

STEP 8

Erase the guidelines and add in details for the eyes and a bit of blush on the cheek. And don't forget a fluffy little deer tail!

Practice drawing the peryton below!

Keep going from step 1.

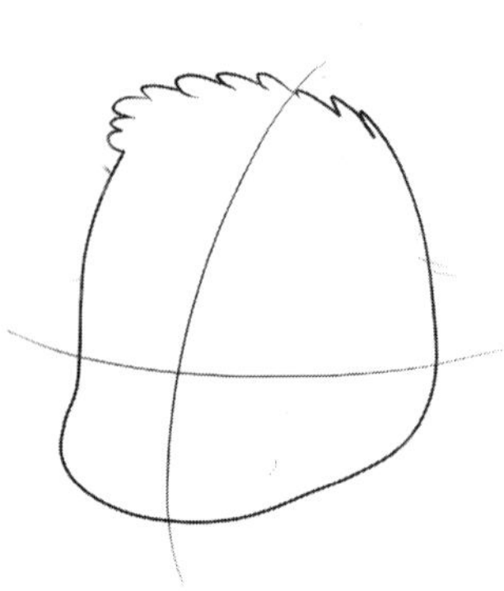

Try a few from scratch.